POWERFUL WOMAN JOURNAL

VOLUME 1

GINNY DYE

A Voice In The World Publishing
Bellingham, WA
www.PowerfulGirlJournals.com
www.AVoiceInTheWorld.com

POWERFUL WOMAN JOURNAL
VOLUME 1

Hello!

You know, it doesn't matter what day of the year you start your journal – it will be with you for 365 days – until you're ready for your next one.

A Journal becomes even more of a treasure when
it becomes even more than a Journal.

The **POWERFUL WOMAN JOURNALS** are so much more than a Journal.

You'll find **POWERFUL WOMAN STORIES** - amazing people who will make you realize you can do ANYTHING with your life. (52 stories for every week of the year)

Every single day you'll get a **POWERFUL WOMAN QUOTE.**

You'll be challenged with **POWERFUL WOMAN ACTIONS.**

And every day you'll have a place to write down your feelings, thoughts, challenges, hurts, disappointments, successes, celebrations, relationships, actions, experiences, adventures – all the things your life is made of.

THE POWERFUL WOMAN JOURNALS WILL BECOME IRREPLACEABLE TREASURES
AS *YOU* LOOK BACK ON *YOUR* LIFE!

Here's the thing... In my many years of working with women I have watched as one after another falters when you reach the "Real World." You start out with such great dreams. You are full of energy and hope - determined to make your mark on the world. Then you face the reality of unkind people; cruel words; failed attempts; unforeseen obstacles; and a myriad of other "Real Life" situations. Your dreams crumble before the onslaught. It doesn't have to be that way! No matter where you are in life – you are weighed down with regrets and disappointments, and you wonder if this is all your life will be.

You will meet incredible people this year, and have the opportunity to meet yourself in a way you probably never have before... You'll become a **POWERFUL** 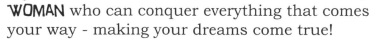 **WOMAN** who can conquer everything that comes your way - making your dreams come true!

If you have a safe place to write down your experiences and all the things you learn along the way – NOTHING will stop you from living the life you dream of right this minute!

It's my honor to be part of your journey with you.

Let's get with it!

Ginny Dye

Before you get started, come over and join our
FACEBOOK Community!

http://www.facebook.com/IAmAPowerfulWoman

Don't miss out on:

Friends
Contests
Games
Videos
Blogs

And one other thing:

Sign up for my mailing list so that you'll get special offers and "Insider Powerful Woman Information" that no one else will get!

Just go to www.PowerfulWomanJournals.com
and join the fun!

POWERFUL WOMAN STORY #1
She's On Her Way!

Eilleen was born in the tiny town of Timmons, Ontario in Canada. She grew up used to bitter cold and hunger. There were days on end when bread and milk was the entire diet for her and her 3 younger siblings. She learned to hide her poverty and hunger from friends at school but it didn't ease the suffering.

About the only thing that could do that was her music. When life was more than she could handle she would retreat to her bedroom with her guitar, singing and writing until her fingers ached. The music fed her soul even while her stomach was growling.

Her talent was recognized early and this little tomboy was shuttled all over to perform in clubs, bars, and anywhere else they could get her booked to make some extra money. Yet Eilleen never really thought music was her future.

When she could no longer stand the poverty she managed to convince her mother to leave their father and head for Toronto. The shelter they stayed in for a long time provided the first regular meals she had ever experienced.

Eilleen got her first job when she was 14, working at a McDonalds. Later, she spent summers working as the foreman of a dozen-man reforestation crew in the Canadian bush, where she learned to wield an axe and handle a chain saw as well as any man. She was tough because she had to be tough.

Then things got tougher. Both parents were killed in an auto wreck and suddenly she was the parent to her siblings. She managed to survive by getting a job singing at a local resort. The experience was invaluable – giving her exposure to every aspect of theatrical performance. It prepared her for what was to come.

In 1990, her siblings were grown and 23 year old Eillen was on her own. The first thing she did was change her first name to an Ojibway Indian name

meaning *"I'm on my way."* **Shania Twain** was indeed on her way. She has turned the world of Country/Pop music upside down, winnig many awards along the way. Unless you live on

5

another planet, you have probably heard of her!

One of her songs, *I'm Gonna Getcha Good,* really sums it up. It's all about a girl who knows what she wants; she not only knows how to get it, but she's going to get it good.

All of us make a choice everyday how we are going to live our lives. No one would have been surprised if little Eilleen had simply become another person sunk in poverty – trapped by the reality of a hard life.

Shania Twain, however, saw her future differently. She was not content to stay where she was – she was determined to pay whatever price necessary to achieve her dreams. Each hard thing did nothing but strengthen her resolve and determination, teaching her how to press through to success!

She learned to do the hard things. She learned how to spot opportunity in every situation. She learned how to ask for what she wanted – and just keep asking until she got where she wanted to be. She learned how to fail, then pick herself back up and do it again.

You can be like Shania!

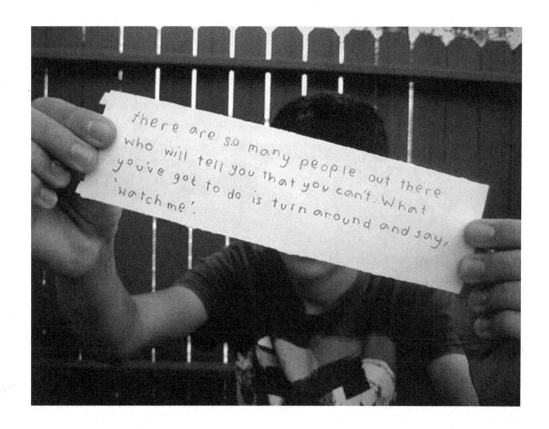

DAY 1: *"Develop an attitude of gratitude and give thanks for everything that happens to you, knowing that every step forward is a step toward achieving something bigger and better than your current situation."* ~Brian Tracy

---

DAY 2: *"No one can make you feel inferior without your consent."* ~ Eleanor Roosevelt

_____

_____

_____

_____

_____

_____

_____

_____

_____

_____

_____

_____

_____

_____

_____

_____

_____

_____

_____

_____

_____

_____

_____

_____

_____

_____

_____

_____

DAY 3: *"It doesn't matter where you have been; it matters where you are going."*

_____

_____

_____

_____

_____

_____

_____

_____

_____

_____

_____

_____

_____

_____

_____

_____

_____

_____

_____

_____

_____

_____

_____

_____

_____

_____

_____

_____

DAY 3: *"It doesn't matter where you have been; it matters where you are going."*

POWERFUL WOMAN ACTIONS

One person can make a difference. In fact, it's not only possible for one person to make a difference, it's essential that one person makes a difference. And believe it or not, that person is you. As we go through this year together I'm going to share ways YOU can make a difference!

READ INDEED

Maria Keller was 4 ½ when she started reading. Her room is lined with bookshelves full of her favorite books – many that she reads over and over. She knows there is something magical about books; that they can take you anywhere you want to go. One day, when she was eight, her mother told her that some kids don't have a single book of her own. She decided to change that!

At age eight she started <u>Read Indeed</u>. She collects books, mostly through drives people hold at their offices or churches, and then distributes them to schools and other groups that help kids in need of a good read. Most of them stay local, but many have been sent all over the world. Her original goal was to donate 1,000,000 books by her eighteenth birthday. It only took her to age 13 to do it!

That's right. 13 year, 7-grader, Maria Keller has given away over 1 MILLION books. Go to her website to find out how YOU can help her or do something just like it in your area! www.ReadIndeed.org

ARE YOU INVOLVED IN A CLUB?

Encourage the club members to choose a project that will make a difference in your community or someone's life. For instance, a Robotics Club designed a special device that enabled a kid stuck in a wheel chair and unable to use his arms, to "throw" balls so he could play fetch with his dog.

FOOD BANK

Help at a food bank or food pantry in your town. There are a lot of people who need a hot meal or some groceries, and you probably have several organizations in your community who provide meals or groceries to folks who need them. Look in your telephone book, or ask a teacher or your religious leader for suggestions. Volunteer with some friends and give a couple hours dishing out food or clearing tables. Help bag groceries, or carry them to the cars. Be sure to smile and talk with the people. They all have the same desires and needs that you do. You just might make a friend or two!

DAY 4: *Anyone or anything that does not bring you alive is too small for you.*
~ David Whyte

DAY 5: *"Successful and unsuccessful people do not vary greatly in their abilities. They vary in their desires to reach their potential."* ~John Maxwell

DAY 6: *"What makes you more powerful than they are is what you can do that they can't, or what you're willing to do that they won't."*

DAY 7: *"Every person dies, but not every person really lives."*

A Victor's Life!

Merri pulled the covers over her head, hoping that if she wasn't seen perhaps her adopted stepmother would ignore her. She could hear birds chirping outside the window. . . if Merri had only been a bird, she could have flown away from the torment a long time ago.

She could hardly remember the years she had been safe and loved. The death of both parents had resulted in her being adopted by her stepmom. Adopted – only to be terribly abused. Fearing the night and dreading the day, Merri could only dream of a safe, free, loving existence.

As she endured and survived, she also vowed that when she was older she would do something to help other adopted children live in safety. She fulfilled her vow... After 30 years in *broadcasting*, Merri Dee serves as Director of Community Relations at WGN-TV in Chicago, Illinois, USA. This enables her to supervise the programs that reach over 55 million homes. She also works as a manager of the TV channel's Children's Charities where over 25 million dollars have been raised. The monies raised have been given solely to children's organizations.

Because of Merri's efforts in raising awareness about the needs of orphans, the adoption rate in Illinois increased over 50 %. Credit is given to her and WGN-TV.

As the host of the United Negro College Fund's annual "Evening of Stars," Merri has helped raise over 30 million dollars for educational scholarships.

These 3 accomplishments are only a small representation of what she has accomplished. Her life is characterized by giving, and giving some more.

Merri lived a lonely and sad life as a child. Neglected and beaten, she knew no love. She could be bitter and angry. But she has taken her desperate past and made her present world better. By doing so, she has made not only her world better, but also the world of thousands of other children.

These feats take on even greater awe when you learn that Merri was kidnapped one night after taping a TV show. Her kidnappers shot her in the head and left her for dead in rural Illinois. She was abandoned, cold and bloody with two bullet holes in her head.

Miraculously, Merri's life-long will and fight to survive came to her rescue

once again and she crawled for help. Finding a nearby highway she managed to flag down a passing car and received the needed medical care that would save her life.

Blinding headaches from the bullet shrapnel still left in her head gives her daily pain. But after more than a year of recovery, Merri returned to the journalistic life she loves.

Her near-death experience fueled a new passion - victim's rights. Merri has been instrumental in getting the first Victims Bill of Rights legislation passed in Illinois. That bill has since become the example for the rest of the USA's victim's legislation.

Today Merri lives a rich fulfilling life. A survivor's life. A life that has its scars on her body and her soul.

But it's a victor's life!

DAY 9 *You will only have joy when you focus on having it and settle for nothing less. ~ Sanaya Roman*

POWERFUL WOMAN ACTIONS

SHARE BEAUTY

If you have flowers in your garden, share them with someone else. Take a bunch to an elderly neighbor who can no longer garden. Take some to a friend going through a hard time. Drop them off at a neighbor's house "just because".

PEOPLE ARE LONELY

Spend an afternoon with someone you know is lonely. You don't have to make it just once. Lonely people are in need of friendship. Decide to drop by every week. Send them notes. Become a lifeline for just that one person.

BE A MENTOR.

Contact Big Brothers Big Sisters, YMCA, or the local elementary schools to find out about mentoring. Meetings can happen at school: in the classroom, school library, school computer room, or other set location. School-based mentoring is not a tutoring program. It's just being a friend to a kid who needs one. Statistics show[4] that kids who are mentored one-on-one in a school setting:
- 58% improved their school performance
- 65% showed higher levels of self-confidence
- 55% had a better attitude toward school

DO YOU LIKE MUSIC OR DRAMA?

Why not volunteer at a local elementary school, YMCA or community center, and put on skits or mini-musicals? You could either enlist teens and perform them for the kids, or better yet, cast the kids in the roles and work with them throughout the year. When they're ready to perform, arrange for a performance in the school auditorium (at the 'Y' or community center). Invite the other classes and parents (and grandparents!). You may foster future artists by "just having fun."

DAY 12   *It is everyone's obligation to put back into the world at least the equivalent of what he takes out.   ~ Albert Einstein*

DAY13 *Far away there in the sunshine are my highest aspirations. I may not reach them, but I can look up and see their beauty, believe in them, and try to follow where they lead. ~ Louisa May Alcott*

PROVIDE SOME CHEER TO SICK KIDS

Do you have a hospital nearby? Maybe even a dialysis center? Often these rooms are a little drab and could use some cheering up! Contact the Pediatrics ward, Oncology (cancer) ward, labs, dialysis center and tell them you'd like to help cheer up their rooms. You can provide cheerful, colorful artwork, DVD movies (you may also need to provide a DVD player), and little care packages. Kids (and probably adults, too) really like the sour Skittles to help with the nasty taste of chemotherapy.

LITTER TEAM

Take your lunch break to clean up trash. Enlist the help of your friends! You'll inspire others to keep your world cleaner and trash free if they see there are people who care.

FAMILY TRASH TEAM

Go out with your family at least 1 hour a week to clean up trash around your neighborhood, on your road, or somewhere else you know needs cleaning up.

BE A SECRET GIVER

Go to your local bowling alley, skating rink, amusement park, etc. and ask them to give you FREE coupons you can share with kids who need to know someone cares. Put the coupons in a special card or note that will let them know they are important.

START A SOUP & CEREAL CAMPAIGN

Did you know you can collect Campbell Soup labels and General Mills box tops for points to purchase things for your school? The school can get things like library books, art supplies, and overhead projectors. Why not challenge all the students, teachers, staff and their families to start collecting? You could even get a van for 1 million soup labels! Don't let all those people throw away all those labels and box tops! Start your campaign today.

DAY 14 *Cautious, careful people always casting about to preserve their reputation or social standards never can bring about reform. Those who are really in earnest are willing to be anything or nothing in the world's estimation, and publicly and privately, in season and out, avow their sympathies with despised ideas and their advocates, and bear the consequences."*
~ Susan B. Anthony

How many times have you been discouraged because someone else didn't see the brilliance of what you created, thought of, or wanted to do? How many times have you walked away from something because you decided it wasn't a good idea, too?

Consider these...

+ The movie Star Wars was rejected by every movie studio in Hollywood before 20th Century Fox finally produced it. It went on to be one of the largest-grossing movies in film history.

+ As a child, Sylvester Stallone was frequently beaten by his father and told he had no brains. He grew up an unhappy loner. He floated in and out of schools. An advisor at Drexel University told him that based on his aptitude tests he should pursue a career as an elevator repair person. It's not a bad profession but it's certainly not where "Rocky" ended up!

+ Einstein was criticized for not wearing socks or cutting his hair. He didn't speak until he was four, and didn't read until he was seven. One observer noted, *"He could be mentally retarded."*

+ An expert said of Vince Lombardi: *"He possesses minimal football knowledge. Lacks motivation."*

+ Beethoven handled the violin awkwardly and preferred playing his own compositions instead of improving his technique. His teacher proclaimed him hopeless as a composer.

+ Walt Disney was fired from his job as a newspaper editor for lack of ideas. He also went bankrupt several times before he created Disneyland.

+ Henry Ford failed and went broke 5 times before he finally succeeded.

+ Louisa May Alcott, the author of Little Women, was encouraged to find work as a servant or seamstress. She would certainly never be a writer.

+ In 1944, the director of the Blue Book Modeling Agency, told modeling hopeful Norma Jean Baker (Marilyn Monroe), *"You'd better learn secretarial work, or else get married."*

+ When Lucille Ball began studying to be an actress in 1927, she was told by the head instructor of the John Murray Anderson Drama School, "Try any other profession. Any other." Hmmm... Where would we be today without *I Love Lucy* reruns??

+ Liv Ullman, who was nominated two times for the Academy Award for Best Actress, failed an audition for the state theater school in Norway. The judges told her she had no talent.

+ Wilma Rudolph was the 20th of 22 children. She was born prematurely and her survival was doubtful. When she was 4 years old, she contracted double pneumonia and scarlet fever, which left her with a paralyzed left leg. At age 9, she removed the metal leg brace she had been dependent on and began to walk without it. By 13 she had developed a rhythmic walk, which doctors said was a miracle.

That same year she decided to become a runner. She entered a race and came in last. For the next few years every race she entered, she came in last. Everyone told her to quit, but she kept on running. One day she actually won a race. And then another. From then on she won every race she entered. Eventually this little girl, who was told she would never walk again, went on to win three Olympic gold medals.

+ Louis L'Amour, successful author of over 100 western novels with over 200 million copies in print, received 350 rejections before he made his first sale. He later became the first American novelist to receive a special congressional gold medal in recognition of his distinguished career as an author and contributor to the nation through his historically based works.

+ In 1953, Julia Child and her two collaborators signed a publishing contract to produce a book tentatively titled *French Cooking for the American Kitchen*. Julia and her colleagues worked on the book for 5 years. The publisher rejected the 850-page manuscript. Child and her partners worked for another year totally revising the manuscript. Again the publisher rejected it. But Julia Child did not give up. She and her collaborators went back to work again, found a new publisher and in 1961 – eight years after beginning – they published *Mastering the Art of French Cooking*, which has sold more than 1 million copies. In 1966, *Time* Magazine featured Julia Child on its cover.

So... *what are your ideas? Your thoughts? Your dreams?* Who cares if anyone supports what you want to do?

The important thing is for YOU to believe. For **you** to ignore the people who say you can't do it – and *do it anyway*! It takes courage. It takes persistence. It takes believing in the "voice inside" when no one else does.

Ideas, dreams, and visions are planted within you because you have the ability to make them happen. You'll learn, grow, scramble, fail, and get back up again. The important thing is to simply never give up. The people I told you about never did – and they made great things happen!

DAY 15 *For what is done or learned by one class of women becomes, by virtue of their common womanhood, the property of all women." ~ Elizabeth Blackwell (The first woman in the U.S. to become a physician)*

DAY 16   *"We've chosen the path to equality, don't let them turn us around."*
~ Geraldine Ferraro (The first woman to be nominated as Vice President of the United States)

DAY 17 *"You can do one of two things; just shut up, which is something I don't find easy, or learn an awful lot very fast, which is what I tried to do."*
~ *Jane Fonda*

WHEELCHAIR SPORTS PROGRAM

Do a little research and find out if there is a wheelchair sports program in your community. There are a lot of fine athletes who are confined to wheelchairs, still active and very competitive. Besides basketball, some wheelchair sports groups play rugby, hockey, tennis and softball. Get some friends together and challenge them to a game. You might be surprised who wins!

HELP JUVENILES HAVE A SECOND CHANCE

Not all kids in juvenile detention centers are bad kids – many times they are kids who made bad choices and got caught. They deserve a second chance; and they deserve to know someone cares. Is there a Juvenile Detention center in your area? Why not contact them and see if there is something you can do for the kids who are incarcerated? It could be collecting gently used paperback books, DVDs, CDs, and/or magazines to donate to the center. Maybe you can get a pen pal group started. Or volunteer to sit on their Board that meets with the juvenile offenders and their guardians to determine the consequences for the youth. You'll have a voice in presenting options to youth and their guardians to help them accept responsibility for their actions and provide accountability to the community and the victim of their crime.

EMAILS OF GRATITUDE

Send at least one email a day telling someone how much they are appreciated; thanking them for something they did for you; or telling them something you like about them.

SHARE SOME JOY!

Not all senior citizens facilities are the same. They vary from having active seniors to bed-ridden individuals. But everybody has the same need – to know someone else cares. Why not throw a party for some folks in such a facility? It can be as simple as just bringing in some balloons and visiting with people (don't worry about what to say – most of them will be happy to do the talking!). Or it can be as elaborate as performing a "show" for them. If you have some friends who play music, sing, can do card tricks, read poetry or tell stories – put it all together and make some people happy! They'll talk about it for weeks. ☺

DAY 18   *"If you have knowledge, let others light their candles in it."*   ~ *Margaret Fuller*

"Don't compromise yourself. You are all you've got." ~ Janis Joplin

33

DAY 20 *"Many persons have a wrong idea of what constitutes true happiness. It is not attained through self-gratification but through fidelity to a worthy purpose."*
~ Helen Keller

_____
_____
_____
_____
_____
_____
_____
_____
_____
_____
_____
_____
_____
_____
_____
_____
_____
_____
_____
_____
_____
_____
_____
_____
_____
_____
_____
_____

It's so easy to look at really successful people and think they just woke up one day that way. Nothing could be further from the truth. Every successful person I know had their share of failures and hardships. The "Queen of Television" was no different...

Born to teenage, unwed parents, Oprah had a lot of things going against her. She was poor, black, a female, and born to parents out of wedlock. Her early years with her grandparents were wonderful, but from age six to thirteen her life was full of abuse and trouble-making. Her mother's failed attempt to put her in a detention center landed her with her father. He helped her turn

her life around and she went on to college and then moved into journalism.

Oprah was fired as a TV reporter because she broke the "cardinal rule" of journalism – remain objective. Oprah started crying while interviewing a woman who had lost seven children in a fire. That show of sympathy cost Oprah her job.

At age 22 and a new anchorperson, she was sitting around a table with men in suits when they suggested she change her name to Suzie. They counseled that it was a "friendlier" and more easily remembered name than Oprah. Oprah rejected their suggestion and decided to stay true to herself.

She knew she was different and liked it that way. So she worked hard to launch her own media career by creating a talk show with heart and a helping hand to people in need. The Oprah Winfrey Show was born. Today Oprah is a one-woman media empire worth billions of dollars.

If Oprah had listened to the "professionals" and followed their advice, I wonder if we'd even know who she is today. But because she rejected the "tested formula" of journalism and built upon her uniqueness, millions of people around the world have been touched and helped because of her.

Each of us is unique, with special gifts and talents. If others recommend you make changes, honestly consider if such changes would diminish who you really are. Some changes might be for the good – others might cause you to compromise your uniqueness. And your uniqueness might just be what the world is waiting for!

DAY 23 *If there is a solution to your problem, then there is little need to worry. If there is NO solution to your problem...then there is little need to worry.* ~ Dalai Lama

_____

_____

_____

_____

_____

_____

_____

_____

_____

_____

_____

_____

_____

_____

_____

_____

_____

_____

_____

_____

_____

_____

_____

_____

_____

_____

_____

_____

_____

If you can't, you must. If you must, you can.

39

COOKIE JAR BANK

Put a big glass jar on your counter. Have everyone in your family (even if it's just you) use it for all their loose change. Every 6 months decide who you are going to give it to – making a family ritual out of the event.

ARE YOU AND SOME OF YOUR FRIENDS "COMPUTER WHIZZES"?

Offer to teach a free class at the YMCA, a church, your school, senior center, or a community center. There are a lot of people who would like to learn about computers but either can't afford to take a class, or are embarrassed to let anyone know they don't understand how to use them. Go slowly and teach one-on-one as much as possible. Make it for all ages – kids through senior adults.

DO YOU LIKE TO HOLD BABIES?

Donate some time at the local hospital in the Pediatrics Nursery. Many hospitals are happy to have volunteers come in and just hold and rock the babies. Or there may be recovery type programs in your area that would appreciate you babysitting while their moms take classes and training.

ARE YOU GOOD AT PHOTOGRAPHY?

Offer your services for free to organizations that need publicity but can't afford to hire professional photographers. It might be a food bank, a homeless shelter, humane society, etc.

VOLUNTEER AT THE LOCAL ANIMAL SHELTER

Many animal rescue groups are short on funding and greatly appreciate any help they can get. They can use help in many areas: cleaning cages, feeding animals, answering phones, doing computer work, etc. The adoration you get heaped on you every day from the animals will give you back more than you can ever give!

DAY 28 *"It is only with the heart that one can see rightly, what is essential is invisible to the eyes."* ~ Antoine de Saint-Exupery

The sun rose and Wilma awoke. Pulling herself together she faced the glowing sunrise. Breathing in the fresh morning air she thought to herself. . . *"No more days watching the old way of life die. No more days feeling the pointed barb of despair."*

Wilma was alive in a time when the Native American culture was at a low point. Want to guess when that was? No, not in the 1700's or even the 1800's but in the 1980's! Less than forty years ago!!!

In fact, Wilma Mankiller is still alive today. Although retired now, her dreams of a time where the men and women of the Cherokee nation returned to the traditional way of working together was very much realized because of her lifelong work.

For the Cherokee, teamwork and working together - both men and woman - for the common good of the whole tribe was a traditional and an honored way of life. However, deep discouragement, broken promises and a completely male dominated culture had replaced their historical ways. Now the women were cast aside and forgotten. They lived hopeless and powerless. And the whole culture fought alcoholism and unemployment.

The year was 1987. Yes, that is right. . . 1987!!! Remember she is the most celebrated Cherokee person in OUR lifetime. . .

Wilma dressed as the morning sun warmed the air. Preparing for her first official day as the elected Chief of the Nation, all of her life's work, hopes and beliefs lay around her mind. Her anticipation of a brighter future began to bubble up.

This day brought the end of much prejudice and ridicule, hardship and skepticism. She dressed and remembered. Wilma knew the sweetness of life could be short.

She remembered the car accident that killed her best friend and nearly killed her. She carries the scars of 17 surgeries. Each scar reminded her as she dressed, that life can only give back to you what you put into it.

She remembered the death threats she received as her popularity with her people grew and the tension grew with her enemies. She remembered buying new tires for her vehicle when its tires were slashed in protest.

She remembered 1985, when she first "inherited" the position as chief of the Cherokee nation. Inherited it because her boss left the position and she was the next in command.

However, this year, 1987, she was freely elected. . . and the very first female ever to hold that position. She knew her people had high expectations for her. She had high expectations. . . for all of them.

As she left for her office, her head held high with pride and hope, she offered silent thoughts of respect for the people who had gone before and deep gratefulness and sincere appreciation for the opportunities ahead of her. She knew her day had finally come. She knew her Nation's day had come as well. Her high expectations, hard work and deep commitment paid off as she was elected twice more as the Nation's chief.

Although her health no longer permits her from officially leading her people, her influence is still felt within the Nation. The Cherokee Nation is a vast organization, with over 140,000 in population, an annual budget of more than $75 million, and more than 1,200 employees spread over 7,000 square miles!!

Wilma's election and her tackling of their problems did much to restore and revive the Cherokee economy, education and equality. She restored faith to a desperate people.

She didn't take the easy way or the quick way. She took the way that was necessary and needed.

So many times we look for the quick way. Wilma is a wonderful reminder that often times it takes a willingness to work within the existing structure. It takes patience to wait for the opportunity that we desire to present itself. But by doing those two things, Wilma created an environment where now, present day young Cherokee girls dream of becoming chief. Before her election, those girls would never have believed that possible.

Today I encourage you to be willing to take the slow road. It just may be the road you are looking for to make that difference in your life. I encourage you to dream like Wilma did of the changes coming.

SEAL OF THE CHEROKEE NATION

"No matter how busy you may think you are, you must find time for reading, or surrender yourself to self-chosen ignorance." ~ *Confucius*

_____

_____

_____

_____

_____

_____

_____

_____

_____

_____

_____

_____

_____

_____

_____

_____

_____

_____

_____

_____

_____

_____

_____

_____

_____

_____

_____

_____

_____

DAY 31 *It is hard to fail, but it is worse never to have tried to succeed.* ~ *Theodore Roosevelt*

SPONSOR A STUFFED ANIMAL TOY DRIVE

You can either request new or gently used stuffed animals. If you get gently used toys, you'll need to wash and line dry them (don't put them in the dryer). Donate them to the Fire Department or Police Department (call ahead to see if they accept them – especially the used toys). Or your local homeless shelters, rehab centers, etc. may like to have them for the children of the people they are caring for.

SAVE A LIFE – SAVE A COMMUNITY – SEND AN ANIMAL

Have you heard of Heifer International (www.HeiferInternational.org)? This is a

very creative way of ending hunger and poverty in communities around the world. Instead of sending money Heifer International sends an animal and teaches the recipient how to take care of it. The person promises to take care of the animal and pass on their animal's offspring to others. They also promise to share their knowledge, resources, and skills with those people. Contact Heifer International for ideas on how to raise funds and choose the kind of animal(s) you'll be sending.

THROW A BIRTHDAY PARTY…

… but instead of gifts ask people to make a contribution to your favorite charity or cause. Better yet, gather friends with birthdays in the same month and see how much you can raise TOGETHER! Invite your entire work force or neighborhood to join you! Do you know someone who has a life-threatening disease? Donate the money to an organization that is researching or helping people with that disease. Maybe you're "into" helping abandoned animals – you can donate the money to your local humane society. It could be you're passionate about the environment – donate "your gift money" to a group like the Sierra Club.

DAY 32   *There is only one success – to be able to spend your life in your own way.*

_____

_____

_____

_____

_____

_____

_____

_____

_____

_____

_____

_____

_____

_____

_____

_____

_____

_____

_____

_____

_____

_____

_____

_____

_____

_____

_____

_____

_____

_____

_____

_____

_____

_____

_____

_____

_____

_____

_____

_____

_____

_____

_____

_____

_____

_____

_____

_____

_____

_____

_____

_____

_____

Volume 1

PEPPER CREST HIGH SERIES

TIME FOR A SECOND CHANCE

Ginny Dye

Kelly thought she left all her problems at home, but did she...?

Volume 2

PEPPER CREST HIGH SERIES

It's Really A Matter of Trust

Ginny Dye

Things were going great for Kelly... with one exception.

IT'S TIME TO DISCOVER THE PEPPER CREST HIGH SERIES!!

WWW.PEPPERCRESTHIGH.COM

For the Teens in your life!

Volume 1

PEPPER CREST HIGH SERIES

A Lost & Found Friend

Ginny Dye

They knew their friend needed help... but what could they do?

Volume 5

PEPPER CREST HIGH SERIES

A Touch of Spring Fever

Ginny Dye

If Greg is the perfect boyfriend, why is Kelly interested in another guy?

DAY 36   *Nothing can stop the woman with the right mental attitude from achieving her goal; nothing on earth can help the woman with the* wrong *mental attitude.*

_____
_____
_____
_____
_____
_____
_____
_____
_____
_____
_____
_____
_____
_____
_____
_____
_____
_____
_____
_____
_____
_____
_____
_____
_____
_____
_____
_____

DAY 36

I'd like to introduce you to the miracle of Chinese Bamboo...

It all begins with a seed – and with the vision of someone willing to wait... A Chinese farmer, usually struggling to survive and provide for his family, plants the seed and sets his hope and vision on all it will provide when it towers 90 feet above his head. With a heart toward the future, he digs hole after hole, plants the seeds, then begins their care. Day after day he carries water to the spots he has marked. And because it's human nature to want to see results he carefully inspects "the spots" every day.

Nothing.

Knowing he has to feed his family he plants other crops, carefully sewn around "the spots" that contain the real hope for his future. He continues to water them every day, feeding them carefully, and watching...

Nothing.

The other crops sprout within weeks, providing nourishment for his family within months, but provide nothing for the future. These crops will not make his dreams come true – they will simply provide for the present. The Chinese Bamboo seeds contain all his hopes, his dreams... A whole year goes by...

Nothing.

He continues to haul water. He stares endlessly at "the spots" but sees nothing but barren ground. His hopes, his dreams, seem so very far away. There is no evidence of life. Has the seed rotted? Has it died before it ever had a chance to grow? Another year goes by...

Nothing.

His neighbors – those who don't know and believe in the miracle of the Chinese Bamboo – laugh at him. They mock his vision for the future. They look on with scorn as he hauls buckets of water to "the spots". He begins to question himself. Will it ever grow? Is he pouring water, and his life's energy, into something that will reap no reward for him?

Another year goes by...

Nothing.

3 years of pouring water, energy and hope into the Chinese Bamboo. Nothing to show for it. Yet he's heard of the miracle of the Chinese Bamboo. He's heard of the huge rewards that come to those who believe. One day he stands over "the spots" and he cries his frustration and fears. "The spots" reveal nothing, the barren ground seeming to mock him, yet the wind whispers hope to him. He sighs and hauls yet more buckets of water.

Another year goes by...

Nothing.

4 years.... 4 years of hoping, wishing, and diligently tending his dream. Surely the miracle will happen now. His neighbors have quit laughing. They no longer even care – yet they talk quietly among themselves of the farmer who "isn't quite right." At this point the farmer isn't even sure... Yet he's fallen into a habit so he continues to water "the spots." He continues to feed them. It's simply what he does now, with no knowledge of reward – just the simple, now unspoken hope that life resides beneath the spots he so carefully tends. Another year passes...

Nothing.

5 years... The farmer is tired. Tired of hauling buckets. Tired of growing and tending so many other crops to feed his struggling family. Tired of trying to keep his dream alive. Tired of seeing no results day after day. He stares hopelessly at "the spots." There can not possibly be life after so many years. He must have watered them wrong. He must not have fed them correctly.

If only he had done things differently, there would be growth. Despair rocks his soul. 5 years he has poured into his dream – into his hope for a better future. His dream mocks him. The vision of a better life for his family melts away under harsh reality. Tears fill his eyes as he grabs for the last hope residing in his soul and slowly lifts the bucket to pour water on to his dream.

After 5 years he realizes it would be folly to give up now...

Then comes the morning when the whole village is jolted awake by the cries of joy from the farmer. They watch startled from their windows as he runs down the dusty road calling for his family to come see. As his family races back up the road after him, the rest of the village pours from their houses to see what has the crazy farmer so excited. They find the family clustered around "the spots", talking excitedly. From the edge of the road they can see green sprouts thrusting out from the barren ground. They seem to be growing before their very eyes! The farmer is dancing.

"The miracle has happened!" he cries.

"The miracle has come!"

"The spots" become the place for everyone in the village to come – watching in amazement as the bamboo grows, and grows, and grows. *5 feet. 10 feet. 20. 30. 40. 50. 60. 70. 80. 90...* In just 6 weeks the bamboo has grown 90 feet tall! 5 years of nothing and now this... 90 feet in 6 weeks! It is truly a miracle!

The farmer stands to the side. He is aware all his dreams have come true. The harvest of the bamboo will provide all he dreamed of for his family. He also realizes the lessons he has learned are far more valuable.

He learned to plant a dream.

He learned to do the daily things that would make it a reality.

He learned to ignore those who said it couldn't happen.

He learned to push past his own fear and doubt and keep taking action.

He learned to have faith when there was no reason to have faith.

Now he smiles every time he walks through the village.

Everyone is hauling buckets of water to their own "spots." Gazing over at his towering 90 feet tall bamboo, they know what can happen.

Because of him.

Because of his willingness to blaze the trail and make his dream come true.

What about you? What are you willing to do to make your dreams come true? How long are you willing to work? How long are you willing to go to school? How much faith and belief are you willing to have? I hope your answer is one that will help you achieve all you dream of in life!

DAY 37 *"I can honestly say that I was never affected by the question of the success of an undertaking. If I felt it was the right thing to do, I was for it regardless of the possible outcome."* ~ *Golda Meir*

DAY 38 *"Something which we think is impossible now is not impossible in another decade."* ~ *Constance Baker Motley (First Black Woman in the U.S. to become a Federal Judge)*

DAY 39 *"I think the key is for women not to set any limits."*
~ Martina Navratilova

SCHOOL GOOD DEED PATROL

Work with your kids to form a "Good Deed Patrol" if you have kids in school. Have them watch for students doing something to make a difference in the school. Tell them to listen to conversations to discover these people. Then talk with your radio station, school newspaper or local newspaper (or all 3!) and ask if they will include a small section in the paper, or a small spot on the radio programs to say THANK YOU to these people. It doesn't have to be much. Think how excited someone would be to open the paper and see a THANK YOU NOTICE to them for something they did. Don't you think more people would want to be noticed by the "Good Deed Patrol"?

COMMUNITY GOOD DEED PATROL

Do the same thing – only take it community, or neighborhood, wide. This could have a huge impact on your community.

NEIGHBORHOOD YARD SALE

Organize your neighborhood around a cause and have a Neighborhood Yard Sale. One neighborhood adopted an orphanage in Thailand and worked together to send thousands of dollars from their garage sale. In addition to the money they sent, neighbors became closer and new friends were made.

BLOW SOMEONE'S MIND

Want to blow someone's mind? Every time someone is rude or mean to you, respond with kindness. One woman was treated very rudely by a co-worker. She responded by taking them a plate of cookies and telling them to have a nice day. Now they go out of their way to be nice to her.

DAY 40 *"I've learned from experience that the greater part of our happiness or misery depends on our dispositions and not on our circumstances."*
~ Martha Washington

_____

_____

_____

_____

_____

_____

_____

_____

_____

_____

_____

_____

_____

_____

_____

_____

_____

_____

_____

_____

_____

_____

_____

_____

_____

_____

_____

_____

_____

DAY 41 *"As a woman I have no country. As a woman my country is the whole world."* ~ *Virginia Woolf*

DAY 42   *A woman is like a tea bag – you can't tell how strong she is until you put her in hot water. ~ Eleanor Roosevelt*

Sandi Watkins was doomed to be a failure.

At least that's what people thought. That's what they said. By the time Sandi got to high school she had the reputation as the biggest trouble-maker in town. She had a long arrest record, mostly for petty crimes, but everyone knew she was on the fast-track to prison.

Teachers cringed when they saw her name on their class list. Sandi was sullen; sat slumped in her seat, and ignored everything going on around her. She had flunked every class in high school but she kept moving up because not one teacher in her school wanted to have her back again. Sandi was moving on - but she was most certainly not moving up.

No one tried to get to know her. Teachers, and most kids, were afraid of her. No one knew when she would erupt with anger, and fights were common. By her senior year, everyone was simply counting the days until Sandi was gone.

Then Sandi did a strange thing. She signed up for a leadership conference that was designed to get students involved in their communities. It was only because she wanted to get out of class, but something happened that first day...

At first she merely stood against the wall and watched with disdain. She would join the discussion groups but only mumbled a few words when it was her turn to speak. But slowly the interactive games drew her in. She really began to open up when her group was asked to make a list of positive and negative things that had happened at school that year. She certainly had some things to add about that.

You could see the surprise on her face when the other kids in the group actually listened to her. She kept talking. Her group told Sandi her ideas made a lot of sense. They began to treat her like a leader. Suddenly everyone realized Sandi was really smart and had some great ideas.

The next day Sandi continued to share her ideas, signing up to be part of the Homeless Project Team. It was clear she knew something about poverty, hunger and hopelessness. No one was more surprised than Sandi when they elected her to be co-chair of the team.

Okay, maybe the teachers were more surprised - *appalled* actually. They insisted Sandi couldn't do it, that it was ridiculous to put something so important into Sandi Watkins' hands. The principal held firm, however - telling them they might be surprised. I'm sure he was hoping he was right.

Sandi and her team put together a Homeless Scavenger Hunt. They went to the Homeless Shelters to find out what they needed most. Then they made a list of things they planned to collect, assigning the most points to those items the shelters needed most. She found out the homeless rarely get dessert, so she gave high points to cookies, brownie & cake mixes, etc. High scores also went for blankets and coats.

Two weeks later, 100 kids hit the streets of their town, followed by support vans to carry their haul. 4 hours later they met back at the school to load everything into a school bus and take it to the shelter.

There was a slight problem, however. By the time the school bus was loaded, there was room for only one person - the driver. Every seat, every square inch of floor, all the way to the ceiling, was packed with what they had collected. Coats, blankets, clothing, food, a lot of desserts - it was the most the Shelter had ever received.

The shelter residents had huge smiles on their faces as they filed out to

help unload the bus. They cheered Sandi and her team. The paper was there to take pictures and tell stories. Sandi was a hero. A leader.

She was definitely a changed person. The rest of her senior year she actually talked in class. She made good grades. She put together 2 more projects for the Homeless Shelter; each time bringing them what they needed most. There were no more arrests.

Sandi graduated in the spring and went on to college - with glowing recommendations from many teachers at her school. Every year she leads 4 projects for the Homeless Shelters in the town where she is a student.

Here is what Sandi has to say, *"I was on the fast-track to nowhere. I was the only one who could change where my life was going. It was scary, but I knew what would happen if I didn't change was worse. I learned I really could make a difference. It changed my whole life. And I learned that other people could believe in me if I only gave them a chance."*

Sandi asked me to share her story to let you know you can be whatever you want to be – and to also tell you kids you may have written off can CHANGE. It's always your choice. She also wanted me to tell you that a little belief goes a long way.

DAY 45 *People often say that motivation doesn't last; well, neither does bathing – that's why it is recommended DAILY.*

DAY 46 *That some achieve great success is proof to all that others can achieve it as well. ~ Abraham Lincoln*

BE A DECORATING ANGEL

Do you like to decorate? Why not start your own interior design company and provide free decorating for low-income families? You can often use items they already have and simply rearrange things to make a room look totally different. Paint isn't expensive, but sure can spruce up a room! If you have friends who prefer working outside, let them do some landscaping while you "design on a dime" inside! This is a great way to build a portfolio AND make a difference!

HELP WILD ANIMALS

Do you love wild animals? You may have an animal sanctuary in your area that

needs help. See if you can work on weekends or during the summer. They need people to help give tours, and help care for the animals. You'll learn about the wild animals' habitats, conservation, and gain a unique insider's view of the animals at the sanctuary.

PARK VOLUNTEER

Do you have a National or State Park nearby? These parks always need a wide variety of volunteers to help with all kinds of projects. How about helping to:

- Support the park's re-vegetation program
- Repair and maintain hiking trail
- Serve visitors in the park's visitor centers

Some projects will take a day, others may be all summer. Enjoy some of our nation's most beautiful country, learn a lot, and make some new friends!

One's best success comes after their greatest disappointments.
~ Henry Ward Beecher

_____

_____

_____

_____

_____

_____

_____

_____

_____

_____

_____

_____

_____

_____

_____

_____

_____

_____

_____

_____

_____

_____

_____

_____

_____

_____

_____

_____

DAY 49 *What would you attempt to do if you knew you would not fail?*
~ Robert Schuller

_____

_____

_____

_____

_____

_____

_____

_____

_____

_____

_____

_____

_____

_____

_____

_____

_____

_____

_____

_____

_____

_____

_____

_____

_____

_____

_____

_____

_____

DAY 50 *Real difficulties can be overcome; it is only the imaginary ones that are unconquerable.*

POWERFUL WOMAN STORY
Infectious!

The spicy meat of the hot dog causes her to roll her eyes and scrunch her face. *"This is soooooo good!"* she manages to squeak out between bites. Her eyes twinkle and her contagious smile is absolutely irresistible. Watching her eat that hotdog makes you drool as she opens wide. . . . and bites.

Rachael loves food, people, and life itself. Her enthusiasm for what she does is as infectious as her wholesome smile. And she's always on the move – it's fun just watching her, she's so down-to-earth, warm, curious and willing to try most anything. She makes the simplest food irresistible.

Rachael Ray's family owned several restaurants on Cape Cod, Massachusetts. She grew up surrounded by food and cooks. Her mother's side of the family came from Sicily and cooked Italian dishes and her father's side of the family was from Louisiana and he cooked Cajun-style.

"Everyone on both sides of my family cooks," she says.

The allure of New York City called to Rachael and success followed. She soon managed a gourmet food market.

Her love of food, fun and family were displayed in everything she touched. . . her warmth and openness oozed out of her market displays and food creations. But while successful and happy, Rachel wasn't content.

As glamorous and exciting as New York City was, Rachael knew she didn't want to spend the rest of her life there, so she moved back home to Lake George, New York. Soon after the move, Rachael became the chef of an upscale gourmet market. Wanting to increase the sales at both the market and the market's in-store restaurant, she used her personal pizzazz and created what we now know as *"30 Minute Meals with Rachel Ray."*

It was so popular that the local CBS station signed her to do a weekly cooking show. *"I did 30 Minute Meals for five years on local television, and I earned nothing the first two years. Then I earned $50 a segment. I spent more than that on gas and groceries, but I really enjoyed making the show and I loved going to a viewer's house each week. I knew I enjoyed it, so I stuck with it even though it cost me."*

And the rest is history. . .

This young woman never attended a culinary training institute, didn't train under a famous chef, nor did she ever work in a five-star restaurant. In fact, she never took a single cooking class. And she is criticized because of it.

Her critics don't think she should be teaching cooking because of her lack of professional credentials and her too-bubbly personality. But Rachael doesn't let it get to her. She says, *"It's all true and I can't do much about it at this point."*

I think that's the key to Rachael's wild success. She doesn't try to be someone she isn't. She's just fun-loving Rachael. And you feel like she's letting you in on some great secrets as she shares with you what she knows and what she's discovered. She includes you in the fun – and that's why people keep coming back to watch her shows.

Rachael keeps everything simple, real and up-beat. But her success was not easy -- she wasn't an "overnight success." She worked hard, stayed open to opportunities and change, walked through doors that opened for her, and stayed true to herself and her values.

Whether she's doing a cooking show, compiling another cookbook, producing her magazine, appearing on her talk show or running her non-profit organization for kids, Rachael keeps it simple, easy and enjoyable.

I hope you'll consider Rachael's "secrets to success" while you work toward your own success. Be real. Be yourself. Keep life simple. Give to others. And have fun!

it Always seems impossible until it's Done.

DAY 51   *Our greatest battles are those with our own minds.*

DAY 53 *The true measure of a person is not how they behave in moments of comfort and convenience, but how they stand at times of controversy and challenges. ~ Martin Luther King*

JUST ONE...

Buy a gift certificate for 1 ice cream cone; 1 Cookie; 1 piece of pie; 1 rose; 1 pizza slice; 1 Video Rental; etc. It doesn't have to be much to make someone feel special. Include a note letting the receiver know how special they are. Just think – not only are you making someone feel special – you are also helping the businesses in your town.

After you've bought several of the "Just 1" Certificates listed above, let the store owner know what you're doing and ask if they will donate some for you to extend what you can give away. Ask around to find out who really needs an extra boost to feel good and make sure the certificates find their way into their hands.

HOMELESS SHELTER SCAVENGER HUNT

Hold a Homeless Shelter Scavenger Hunt. You'll need a group of people – the more the better. Next, call a Homeless Shelter and ask for a list of needs, asking them to put the ones they need most, or get the least of, at the top of the list. Assign points to each item – with the most needed items getting the most point value.

Now send everyone out with their list – letting them know that the team, or the person, that creates the most points with what they bring in will win the Contest. Either put up a prize yourself or ask a local restaurant if they will provide a Free meal to the winners.

Collect everything and take it to the Shelter.

TOY DRIVE

Do a Toy Drive for your local Battered Women's Shelter or Homeless Shelter if it has kids. They don't have to be new. Go around your neighborhood and ask each family to donate the "in good condition" toys their kids don't use anymore. There will be tons!

DAY 55 *In order to discover new lands one must be willing to lose sight of the shore for a very long time.*

DAY 56 *She who is not courageous enough to take risks will accomplish nothing in life.*

Everyone knew it couldn't be done.

Roger Bannister had no real motivation to prove them wrong. The young Englishman loved to run, but from the time he was a child he also had a passion to be a doctor. This was the passion that drove him. His parents were unable to afford a University education so it was up to him to make it happen.

He knew early on that to achieve his dream of being a doctor he would have to be exceptional – so he set about being exceptional. His studies were paramount but that didn't mean he couldn't improve his track skills by running to and from school. While he was on his way to earning a scholarship from Oxford University, he was also gaining a name for himself as a runner.

"It is physically impossible for a human being to run a mile in under 4 minutes." This statement was the accepted wisdom of the time during the late 1940's and early 1950's. Runners tried, but failed, proving the words of athletes and medical doctors – cementing a belief in runners' minds that it couldn't be done.

Roger didn't set out to prove them wrong. He simply loved to run and he was fast. He was also learning a lot about the human body in his studies at Oxford. The day arrived when he was firmly convinced it WAS possible for a human being to run the mile in under 4 minutes.

His decision to be that person was formed by a humiliating defeat in the 1952 Olympics. In order to redeem himself he decided to break the world's record for the mile. No one believed he could do it.

Adding to his challenge was the fact he was now a full-time medical student and he could devote only 45 minutes a day to training. People scoffed at the idea he could accomplish such a wild goal but Roger believed slow and steady training would allow him to break the record. He painstakingly researched mechanical aspects of running, and developed scientific training methods to help him achieve his goal.

His opportunity came 2 years later – on a blustery day with 25 MPH gusts of wind to hamper his efforts. It didn't look promising. So what? He had trained. He was ready. He *believed* it could be done.

So he simply went out and did it. Roger ran the race of his life, breaking the tape and collapsing as the announcer delivered his time to a wildly cheering crowd:

3:59.4

Within two months his record had been broken by John Landy – proving the 4 minute mile was as much a psychological barrier as it was a physical barrier. As the years have passed the mile has been run in shorter and shorter times but it was Roger Bannister who proved the body was capable of far more than people believed.

When he was asked to explain that first four-minute mile – and the art of record breaking – his answer was simple: "It's the ability to take more out of yourself than you've got."

Did you get that?

"It's the ability to take more out of yourself than you've got."

How did Roger do it? First, he BELIEVED he could do it. He understood the size of his success would be determined by the size of his belief.

Here is where I'm going to depart from some more common thoughts that are spread around a lot today. While belief is critically important – in fact, he couldn't have accomplished what he did without it - belief alone is not enough. It is not enough to repeat affirmations over and over to yourself, even though they are important.

At some point you have to do the *work*. Roger Bannister ran day after day. He researched the human body. He created scientific methods to enable him to stretch his limits. He did what it would take to fulfill his dream.

What are your goals? What is it you dream of accomplishing? **BELIEVE it can be done. Then do the work. Apply yourself to success. Apply yourself to excellence. Figure out what it is going to take and then go DO IT!**

You may have no interest in breaking a world record, but I believe you have an interest in being the best you that you can be!

DAY 58 *Far better it is to dare might things, to win glorious triumphs even though checkered by failure, than to rank with those poor spirits who neither enjoy nor suffer much because they live in that gray twilight that knows neither victory nor defeat. ~ Theodore Roosevelt*

DAY 59   *So go ahead and make mistakes. Make all you can. Because that's where you will find success – on the far side of failure. ~ Thomas J. Watson*

DAY 60 *We learn wisdom from failure much more than from success; we often discover what will do by finding out what will not do; and probably she who never made a mistake never made a discover.* ~ Samuel Smiles

HELP THEM STAY IN THEIR HOMES!

Help low-income elders and disabled adults keep their dignity and stay in their homes. Volunteer to help
- Drive clients to the grocery store or to medical appointments
- Run errands and go shopping
- Help with the housework or yard work
- Cut and/or deliver wood for heating
- Assist them with moving or packing
- Read to them, write letters for them, make phone calls for them

Many people cannot afford to pay for such services, don't qualify for assistance, or don't have family or friends to help out. Contact your local volunteer center if you need help finding someone. They will be thrilled!

SUMMER CHORES SERVICE

Start a Summer Chores Service – getting friends and kids to help. Gather some friends together who will volunteer to help elders or disabled people. What would it be like to be confined to a wheel chair and have your overhead light go out? It won't be hard to get a list of people who need help. Can you. . .
- Clean a gutter?
- Fix a leaky faucet?
- Change a light bulb?
- Wash windows?
- Mow the lawn?
- Paint a wall?
- Vacuum a carpet?

They may be small chores, but they all add up when you're all alone and can't keep up with them!

DOG WALKER

Volunteer to walk dogs. Animal shelters, homebound people, and people on vacation are just some of the people who may need help with their dogs. Happy dogs make happy people, and nothing makes dogs happier than going for walks (or playing with their favorite toys).

DAY 61   *A life spent in making mistakes is not only more honorable, but more useful than a life spent doing nothing. ~ George Bernard Shaw*

DAY 62 *There are two mistakes one can make along the road to truth – not going all the way, and not starting. ~ Buddha*

Success if going from failure to failure without losing your enthusiasm.
~ Winston Churchill

Jim struggled. *"Put on the glove. Catch the ball. Take off the glove. Throw the ball. . . . "*

Jim's family struggled silently from the sidelines as well.

Jim kept on. *"Put on the glove. Catch the ball. Take off the glove. Throw the ball."*

As little Jim grew up his desire was to play sports. His parents and family watched in agony as his determination grew with each mistake made. The sun and sweat of the playing fields didn't make learning or watching any easier. In team sports, each player is essential. Each position sets up the next player for success or failure. One dropped ball can mean failure for the entire team. Each player needs to be able to fully play his position and help take care of the next player. Jim knew he had to figure out a way to be a true team player.

Jim kept trying. *"Put on the glove. Catch the ball. Take off the glove. Throw the ball. Put on the glove. Catch the ball. Take off the glove. Throw the ball."*

Finally he found a system that worked. . . you see, Jim was born with only one hand and Jim loved sports. . . especially football and baseball. He simply wanted to play. He didn't know why he couldn't. He could throw and catch. He just had to do it differently than 2 handed kids. I guess no one thought to tell him you can't play these sports very long with only one hand.

FINALLY, Jim mastered that *"Put on the glove... Catch the ball... Take off the glove... Throw the ball..."* technique.

Jim started figuring out how to do what he wanted when he was only 4 years old!!! Why so young? Because he wanted to play -- pure and simple. To Jim, only having one hand meant nothing more than doing things differently from everyone else.

Looking over Jim Abbott's many sports accomplishments and *professional* sports awards (including being the pitcher on the U.S. OLYMPIC baseball team) you will read:

. . . *"Starting quarterback on his high school football team which went to the finals of the Michigan state championship...went to the University of Michigan on a baseball scholarship...led the U of M Wolverines to 2 Big Ten titles...won the prestigious Golden Spikes Award, the U.S. Baseball Federation's Golden Spikes awards, awarded (twice) Michigan's Most Valuable Pitcher...won gold medal in the 1988 Olympics...and the list goes on and on.*

Yet when you listen to Jim speak, it is to hear a thankful man with a big heart who loves to share the lessons he has learned from his life experiences. He gives back to kids and to life every time he sees the opportunity.

Retired from professional sports now, Jim's reputation as a public speaker is one of respect and courage.

Do you know what he says about who is responsible for whatever good he has done? It's always the people in his life who BELIEVED he could...his parents, family and friends. He speaks often of that simple truth, *"they believed in me... so I believed in me."*

No one ever told him he couldn't and he just never realized that he *shouldn't* be able to do the stuff he did. How about you? Can you justify NOT doing what you love? I know I can't.

It is not about what life gives you that makes a difference, it is what you DO with what life gives you that makes a difference.

Don't quit just because you feel like a one-handed ball player. Keep figuring out how to do it differently because you will succeed if you don't stop!!

"The will to win, the desire to succeed, the urge to reach your full potential... these are the keys that will unlock the door to personal excellence."
~Eddie Robinson

DAY 65 *I honestly think it is better to be a failure at something you love than to be a success at something you hate.* *~ George Burns*

DAY 66 *She who has never tasted what is bitter does not know what is sweet.*
~ German Proverb

DAY 67 *Whatever the mind can conceive and believe; it can achieve! ~ Napoleon Hill*

POWERFUL WOMAN ACTIONS

CLOTHING BANK ANGEL

Is there a clothing bank in your community? Volunteer to help sort and hang donated items. You might also be able to help customers find items, or help the organization with their mailings, answering phones, doing clerical work (typing, filing, etc.).

FOREIGN EXCHANGE HOST

Be a host family for a foreign exchange student. Nothing promotes world peace, breaks down cultural barriers, and promotes understanding than getting to know someone from a different country. Hosting a foreign exchange student is a challenge, but is well worth it because you end up having a friend for life in another part of the world!

NOTHING IS EVER WASTED

You can make a huge difference for your Food Bank or Homeless Shelters by setting up a route of restaurants and grocery stores – picking up the food they are going to throw away. That's right! Restaurants have to throw away any food left at the end of the night. Help them make a difference by picking it up and taking it to people who are hungry. Grocery stores have to throw out what is expired. Call them and ask what you have to do to be able to pick up the food on a regular basis – perhaps parents can help if school presents a scheduling problem.

NEIGHBORHOOD GARDEN

Grow your own food... to SHARE. Start in your own neighborhood. If you've got the space, start a neighborhood garden. Everyone who helps with it gets to share the produce. If you can, plant fruit trees that will continue to produce for generations to come. If you have extra take it to a local homeless shelter, women's shelter, or food bank.

** Important: **KEEP IT ORGANIC!**

Want to go BIGGER? Find a local business who has space, or an empty lot you can turn into a BIG Garden. Enlist all your friends to help through the Spring & Summer – distributing the food to people in need, and also providing fresh, organic food for your own families. There's nothing like eating food you've grown yourself.

DAY 68 *In the confrontation between the stream and the rock, the stream always wins – not through strength, but through persistence.*

DAY 69 *In the absence of clearly defined goals, we become strangely loyal to performing daily acts of trivia.*

How much courage does it take to follow your passion? *Ask Bethany Hamilton...*

Bethany, who lives in Hawaii, was in grade school when she started her quest to become a professional surfboarder. Surfing is her passion. She spent every available minute in the water; even homeschooling so she would have more time to pursue her goal. When she was 8 years old she entered her first major competition and eventually took the division championships that year. This girl obviously had what it took.

It was almost all taken away from her on Halloween morning, 2003. Bethany was 13 years old. She was surfing with her best friend, Alana, and Alana's brother and father. The waters were calm, not good for surfing, so Bethany was just lying on her board, her left arm dangling in the cool water.

She remembers a flash of gray, a lot of pressure, and a couple fast tugs. She also remembers watching the jaws of a 15-foot tiger shark cover the top of her board and her left arm. She watched in shock as the water around her turned bright red.

The shark was gone as fast as it appeared. So was her arm – bitten off almost to the armpit.

Bethany was horrified, but not in pain at that point. She yelled to her friends and their father, Holt. *"I just got attacked by a shark!"*

It was a combination of miracles that saved Bethany at that point. High tide allowed them to make it over the reef without going around. Holt knew enough to wrap his shirt around the wound to act as a tourniquet while they paddled the quarter-mile to shore. While Bethany drifted in and out of consciousness, a nearby vacationer who was a paramedic, rushed to help her.

Surgery saved her life but her arm was gone for good; and everyone, Bethany included, thought her surfing days were over. Balance is everything when surfing. How could she balance with only one arm?

Within a week, spurred by her passion for surfing, Bethany was thinking something different. **I can do it. I know I can do it!** She wasn't ready to give up what she loved so much, but it would take time for her body to heal.

There was a huge outpouring of love and support from Hawaiians and people all over the world. Love, food, flowers, cards, money... Bethany gathered hope and courage from the waves of love aimed toward her.

It was only a few weeks later – the morning before Thanksgiving - when Bethany headed back for the water. Her love of surfing wouldn't let her wait any longer. Her family and friends were there to cheer her on when she stepped into the warm water for the first time since the attack. It was like coming home.

Bethany smiled and waved, then jumped on her board to paddle out – pushing down the fear of what might be waiting under the water. *She knew too well...*

She failed at her first attempts to ride the board, struggling to push herself up with one arm and keep her balance. Tears rolled down her face, and the crowds cheered when she caught her first wave and rode it in. **Bethany was back!**

Really back. Only months after her vicious incident, Bethany amazed thousands by achieving the unimaginable; taking 5th at the 2004 National Scholastic Surfing Association Nationals Championships. That September she struck again, winning the Open Women's Division of the NSSA's Hawaiian conference season opener. After placing in the finals of the National Surfing Championships, Bethany secured a spot on USA's National Surfing Team.

Ask Bethany if she is afraid of sharks and she'll say yes. Her heart pounds when she sees a shadow in the water. She has nightmares. But she also has a dream, and moving beyond her fears is the only way to accomplish her dreams – the only way to fulfill the passion she has for surfing.

Is there a fear keeping you from following your passion? I would encourage you to do what Bethany has done. Stare it in the face, acknowledge you are afraid, then go out and do it anyway!!

DAY 72 *If you learn only methods, you'll be tied to your methods; but if you learn principles you can devise your own methods. ~ Ralph Waldo Emerson*

DAY 73 *You see things and say, "Why?", but I dream things and say "Why not?" ~ George Bernard Shaw*

DAY 74 *Motivation is like food for the brain; you cannot get enough in one sitting. It needs continual and regular feeding.*

COMPUTER MOUSE DONATIONS!

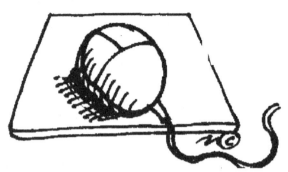

Use the click of your computer mouse to donate free food, help save the rainforests, buy books for kids, rescue animals (and more) – really! Go to The Hunger Site (www.TheHungerSite.com) and use the tabs across the top of the site to make your "donation." All you do is click the big button under the picture and the companies who have volunteered to make contributions do so according to how many clicks are received each day.

When you click the button, you'll be told what your click did. For instance, for the rescue animals it says: *"Thank You! Your click provided the value of .6 bowls of food and care to a rescued animal in a shelter or sanctuary."* You can click once a day in each area – so get your friends together and remind each other to "make your donation clicks" every day! Put it into your mobile as a reminder!

GET YOUR KIDS INVOLVED IN THE WORLD

There are hundreds of links at www.Freechild.org/issues.htm for ideas from Creativity issues to Education issues to Democracy issues, Rights issues, Youth issues, Social issues and much, much more. Use these ideas to jump-start your own creative thinking. Be sure to visit the Actions section to see what projects youth are heading up and leading! The site says: *The Freechild Project has found that young people across the nation are leading their communities in activism for social change.* Help your kids be a positive force in your community!

SAVE THE ENVIRONMENT!

Are you interested in saving the environment? We have a free eBook entitled 101 Ways to Help Planet Earth which you can download at www.TogetherWeCanChangeTheWorld.com.

You can also find many, many resources on the Sierra Club website (www.SierraClub.org) including their new Sierra Club Radio where they offer tips and tell stories you can use as a consumer, citizen, and neighbor for making responsible choices and connect to the growing environmental community. (www.SierraClubRadio.org) You can listen via their mp3 file or subscribe to their free podcast.

DAY 75 *Shoot for the moon. Even if you miss, you'll land among the stars.*
~ Les Brown

_____

_____

_____

_____

_____

_____

_____

_____

_____

_____

_____

_____

_____

_____

_____

_____

_____

_____

_____

_____

_____

_____

_____

_____

_____

POWERFUL WOMAN STORY
Evita

Eva delighted in the love and cheers of the crowd. She couldn't believe it was all for her. "I've come such a long way," she thought to herself. As she smiled and waved to the sea of faces in the courtyard below, she let her mind float back over time. . .

Eva Ibarguren Duarte was born in 1919 as the fifth child to an unwed mother. Although the law frowned upon illegitimate children, it wasn't unusual for wealthy men to have several families in rural areas of Argentina at that time.

When Eva was one year old, her father returned to his legal family, leaving Doña Juana Ibarguren and her family impoverished. All Juan Duarte left to his "illegitimate" family was a document declaring the five children were his so they could bear his last name. Doña Juana was reduced to living in the poorest part of town. She supported her children by sewing clothing for neighbors.

Eventually Eva's older brother moved the struggling family into a larger house which they turned into a boarding house and restaurant. It was during this time that Eva became enthralled with acting and participated in all of her school's plays and concerts.

She still shudders at the memory of her mother's plans for marrying her off to one of the boarders in their house. Eva begged and cajoled her mother to allow her to go to the big city of Buenos Aires. *"Mama, please – there is no future for me here,"* she pleaded. Eva's mother finally gave in and accompanied her daughter to the big city where Eva was hired as an actress at a radio station.

Changing her name to Evita, she spent the next 9 years working in radio productions, as well as the theater, doing some modeling, and making movies. But radio (there was no TV in Argentina yet) was where she thrived, and she became one of the highest paid radio actresses in Argentina.

Evita was suddenly pulled from her reverie. The crowd was chanting her name. She lifted both hands to her mouth and dramatically threw kisses to the adoring throng. Their roar dimmed as she remembered the first time she saw her husband – the man whose side she'd never left for the past 7 years.

A devastating earthquake had mobilized Colonel Juan Perón, Secretary of Labor, to establish a fund for the victims. As a fundraiser, he organized an "artistic festival" and invited radio and film actors to participate. It was during these festivities that Juan Perón met and fell in love with Eva Duarte and they became inseparable.

Eva and Juan were married in December 1945, the year the Labor Party chose Perón as their candidate for President. For the very first time in Argentina's history, a candidate's wife campaigned and traveled with him. At each stop along the campaign trail, Eva handed out buttons and personally greeted the people. She even represented him when he was too ill to speak.

When Perón assumed the Presidency, unlike other first ladies, Evita chose to take an active political role. She immersed herself in serving her country devoting her tireless energy to the disadvantaged, the working class, the elderly, children, and women (she was instrumental in getting them the vote in 1951).

In 1950, Evita was diagnosed with cancer, but she refused to slow down. She created medical clinics for the workers, and distributed subsidies to the poor, as well as clothing, food and household goods. She created entire

neighborhoods of affordable housing, school food programs, jobs for the unemployed, equipment for hospitals, water and sanitary facilities for low income neighborhoods, and pensions for people over 60. (This is just a tiny, tiny list of her vast accomplishments.) *Evita became a legend in her own time.*

At age 33, Evita died of cancer. While there is a great deal of legend, myth and misinformation circulating about this driven woman, no one can deny the passion she had for her country and the incredible work she did on its behalf.

Evita never forget what it felt like to be poor. She knew what it meant to work hard. She understood how it felt to be discarded, criticized and degraded. But when she found herself in the position of being able to make a difference for others, she threw herself into it with all she had. What she accomplished in seven short years was remarkable.

You are not expected to do what you cannot do – you are only responsible for doing what you can. When you find yourself in the position of being able to stand up and make a difference, be like Eva Perón and do everything you can to make it happen. Like a song says, *"It's not who you knew, it's not what you did, it's how you lived."* By living with passion and purpose you can't help but be a POWERFUL WOMAN!

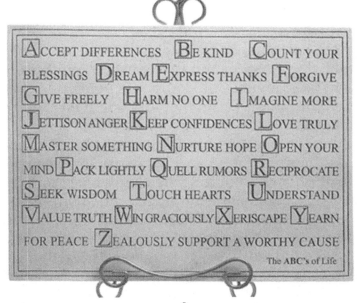

Accept differences Be kind Count your blessings Dream Express thanks Forgive Give freely Harm no one Imagine more Jettison anger Keep confidences Love truly Master something Nurture hope Open your mind Pack lightly Quell rumors Reciprocate Seek wisdom Touch hearts Understand Value truth Win graciously Xeriscape Yearn for peace Zealously support a worthy cause

The ABC's of Life

DAY 80 *Snowflakes are one of nature's most fragile things, but just look what they can do when they stick together.*

DAY 81 *Don't be afraid your life will end; be afraid that it will never begin.*
~ Grace Hansen

CAN'T DECIDE?

Having trouble coming up with a project to pour your heart and soul into? Go to www.ServiceLinkNW.org and they'll take you through the process step by step. Start with the Focus section to figure out exactly what you're passionate about -- what "pushes your buttons." From there they lead you through the Planning, Action and Learning stages of your project.

Get some friends together and go through it as a group. You'll be amazed at what you'll discover about yourself, your community and the power you really do have to make positive changes!

STOP POLLUTION!

Got a polluted stream, creek or river in your area? Pull together some friends and start cleaning it up. If you notice foam, there may be some pollutants getting into the water. Take water samples in several locations up and down the stream and then take them to your local high school science lab teacher or local environmental agency to get the measurements of toxicity and what the toxins are. Then gather the resources (including people, the media, etc.) that you need to clean up the pollution sources.

MAKE IT PERSONAL!

Is there a jail, prison or rehabilitation center nearby? Many of these people will have children at home missing their mom or dad. Make arrangements to take a tape recorder and some children's books into the prison or center and have the parent read the stories as if they're reading them to their own kids. Then send the tape and books to their kids so they can hear their mom or dad read to them.

DAY 84 *Behold the turtle... He only makes progress when he sticks his neck out! ~ James Bryant Conant*

She picks up the small stone and admires the bright colors. *"How much do you think we should ask for this one?"* she asks her friend. They bicker for a while, and then come to an agreement just in time.

"Hurry! Look! Here comes someone!"

9 ½ year old Janine and a friend were selling their artwork (painted rocks) at a roadside stand to raise spending money. But something happened when the money started coming in – the two girls decided to put their money where it mattered, saving the rainforest around their town.

When Janine Licare was 4 years old her family moved to Manuel Antonio, Costa Rica, a beautiful area of rainforest and wildlife. *"Ever since we were little, we acknowledged the fact that it is home to many kinds of animals as well as other living organisms such as trees, plants and insects. The rainforest is an amazing place and we vow to do anything and everything we can to save it. . . If it disappears, then so does our planet."*

The girls created a non-profit organization and opened a store, *Kids Saving the Rainforest* (KSTR), in a corner of a local hotel restaurant. Nine years later, that little corner shop turned into a successful store selling donated artwork and merchandise to raise funds for KSTR's numerous projects. The store also distributes information about their organization, and important environmental issues affecting their area. 100% of the profits go directly to KSTR and Janine's ongoing quest for saving their local rainforest.

One of the first projects *Kids Saving the Rainforest* tackled involved the native, and endangered Titi (squirrel) monkeys, which were dying at an alarming rate. With some investigation, the girls discovered two problems. One problem was that the monkeys were being hit by cars as they tried to cross the roads. The other, was the monkeys were being electrocuted trying to cross over the roads on power lines.

To address the problems, KSTR instituted monkey bridges which are ropes stretched high above the roads so the animals could safely cross. Over 120 such monkey bridges have been installed with the help of the local hydroelectric company, and local experts. The bridges are maintained by *Kids Saving The Rainforest* (KSTR).

Janine is also busy helping plant indigenous trees around the town in which the monkeys and other wildlife feed and live. So far they have planted over 5,000 trees which were also in danger of extinction.

Janine had yet another idea. Why not sponsor a kids' camp every Saturday where she and others teach children about the rainforest, its destruction, and how to help save it? *"Kids are the future. We are the generation that will have to make a difference. Everything depends on us,"* says Janine. Some of the artwork created by the children attending these camps is sold in the KSTR store.

Janine has been instrumental in other projects as well:
- creating a website
- raising money for and purchasing property for an animal rehabilitation center
- a gift shop that sells artwork created by kids and local people
- a program within the community teaching about why NOT to feed the monkeys
- a public library (the first in the area) with over 2000 books people can borrow.
- publishing 3 children's books
- developing sister schools in Denmark, Pakistan, England, Viet Nam, France, Canada, India, the U.S.A. and Costa Rica.

Janine says, *"With the help of volunteers, friends, classmates and the community, we've gone a long way. I believe kids can make a real difference."*

Although Janine was only 9 ½ years old when she and a friend got the idea of selling painted rocks to help save the rainforest, she didn't consider age a factor against them. They started asking for help until they found it!

Janine has remained a major force behind all KSTR's projects. With the assistance of her board of directors, and generous volunteers, Janine is truly making a difference in her world. (You can visit her website at: www.KidsSavingTheRainforest.org.)

What does it take to make a big difference? It means taking one step at a time. Janine didn't start out with a successful organization; she started out selling painted rocks at a roadside stand. Each question she asked and each request for help was a single step along her pathway to success.

Don't think you have to start out big – as the saying goes, *"the trip of a thousand miles begins with the first step."* Be like Janine and get started on your trip to success today!

YOU CAN DO IT!

Go to www.kidssavingtherainforest.org to learn more!

DAY 86 *The purpose of life is not to be happy. It is to be useful, to be honorable, to be compassionate, to have it make some difference that you have lived and lived well. ~ Ralph Waldo Emerson*

IT'S TIME TO DISCOVER THE...

WWW.THENITTYGRITTYCLUB.COM

For the Tweens & Teens in your life...

This exciting new series features Powerful Girls from every state in the United States who have to face the challenges and danger of discovering the Nitty-Gritty Truth in situations most would walk away from. They choose to walk *into* the danger – facing whatever they have to in order to find and expose the TRUTH.

DAY 87 *It's the action, not the fruit of the action, that is important. You have to do the right thing. It may not be in your power, may not be in your time, that there will be any fruit. But that doesn't mean you stop doing the right thing. You may never know what results come from your action. But if you do nothing, there will be no result. ~ Mahatma Gandhi*

DAY 88 *I am only one; but still I am one. I cannot do everything, but still I can do something; I will not refuse to do something I can do. ~ Edward Hale*

EASE TENSIONS

Are there tensions between cultural groups in your community? Why not reach out and help cross the divide through area schools? Invite a school's drama class to join with another and perform a play that will help build bridges. A terrific play, *To Kill A Mockingbird*, would be an excellent choice. It may be a little awkward at first when your two schools get together, but you'll find that by working together and performing such a play will help your community and it will open up a whole new world for everyone involved!

START A HAM RADIO OR AMATEUR RADIO CLUB

Computers aren't the only way to communicate with people from around the world. More and more schools are installing and setting up these radios. Ask your science teacher or a local ham radio club to help you. You'll need to take some tests to earn your operator's license. Then you'll be able to talk with other operators around the world.

INTERNATIONAL MISSIONS

Organize a volunteer mission trip to another country. There are many organizations that can help connect you with people who need you. Just one such organization is i-to-i Volunteer Organization (www.i-to-i.com) where you can get help connecting to volunteering opportunities, internships and more.

The i-to-i organization works with local charities, government bodies and community organizations to help find volunteers. You can choose the type of work you want to do: community development projects, conservation projects, teaching projects, building projects, or teaching English.

_____
_____
_____
_____
_____
_____
_____
_____
_____
_____
_____
_____
_____
_____
_____
_____
_____
_____
_____
_____
_____
_____
_____
_____
_____
_____
_____
_____
_____
_____

DAY ११ *Be who God meant you to be and you will set the world on fire.*
~St. Catherine of Siena

DAY 92 *What we do for ourselves dies with us. What we do for others and the world, is and remains immortal.*

At first glance, the pizza looks and tastes like most home delivery pizza.

Hot, cheesy, and wafting of oregano and parmesan, Domino's Pizza has kept many a student going!!! I don't think there is a teenager around who hasn't eaten their pizza.

But did you know founder Tom Managhan has donated hundreds of MILLIONS of dollars? HUNDREDS of millions! He also made some big mistakes in his life... but he didn't quit!

"But Mom, I want to come home. I don't want to be here at the children's home."

"But Mom, I'm sorry. I was just having fun at seminary. I didn't know the nuns would kick me out for that!"

"But Mom, I'm sorry! I thought I was joining the Army. Yes, I know how tough the Marines really are!"

"But Mom, James <u>wanted</u> to trade the store for the VW!"

These conversations could have taken place in Tom's life. His mother loved him, but because she could not care for him, she took him to a Catholic children's home. He did get expelled from seminary; did accidently join the wrong branch of the U.S. military; and did trade his brother a VW Beetle for his brother's half of a little known pizza restaurant.

However, what I learned after taking a second glance at Tom Managhan's life was the millions of dollars he has invested, donated, and given away... despite his mistakes. He took each large mistake he made and tried again.

That is the key to success you know -- trying and trying again!

While still in college, he and his brother James bought a little pizzeria in Michigan. Tom worked and worked and worked that little business until it was the DOMINO'S PIZZA EMPIRE.

Then he was able to buy and sell land, furniture and even entire professional baseball teams with MILLION dollar price tags.

But even with his affluence Tom wasn't very happy deep inside. He knew he was missing something, so he took a break, a 2 year hiatus from work. He re-examined his purpose, his passions, and his beliefs.

He wound up a different man. His "reawakening" brought him peace. Purpose. Meaning. He discovered **he had more by giving to others.** So he channeled his business savvy and talent into more philanthropic endeavors.

He sold his pizza business and now spends his life creating, funding, building, supporting, and sustaining businesses, colleges, investments and communities that he feels best represent his personal beliefs.

Tom didn't allow being given up as a child, his mistakes or his disillusionment with life to stop him from living. He took the punches, the failings and kept on going. Not everyone in this world agrees with his new directions. They question his religious zeal. The business world wonders at his new enthusiasm. But Tom knows he has to do what gives him the most inner peace.

I wonder; do you know that you too need peace? You don't have to have millions of dollars to give away to find it. All you have to do is to ask yourself, *"Is what I am doing bringing me peace?"*

It doesn't matter how old you are - your honest answer will reveal much. I sincerely hope if you don't have that calming power of peace in your life that you do whatever it takes to get it. I know it is not easy, nor does it happen overnight. But one small step today will bring you a little closer to it tomorrow.

Next time you take a bite out of a Domino's pizza, remember the man who didn't do it all correctly, but kept on trying until he made it right!

"I feel all these setbacks were tools for me to learn from. I used them as steppingstones and didn't see them as failures. A failure is when you stop trying, and I never did that."

~ Tom Monaghan

DAY 93   *Courage is the most important of all the virtues because without courage you can't practice any other virtue consistently.*   ~ Maya Angelou

The best way out is always through. ~ Robert Frost

DAY 95 *You never know what's around the corner. If could be everything. Or it could be nothing. You keep putting one foot in front of the other, and then one day you look back and you've climbed a mountain.*

JOIN AN ARCHEOLOGICAL DIG

It can be so cool to discover what is in your very own area – giving you a glimpse into the past. See if you have a "dig" happening in your area (call your local college or historical society). Many communities do have digs happening because of construction that has uncovered artifacts. Here's an opportunity to "touch history" in a unique and important way. You might find you extend out to other places in your country or around the world.

PLANT A TREE!

Fight global warming by planting a tree – or lots of them. They produce oxygen and give birds homes and provide food for wildlife. They also cool your home and neighborhood, break the cold winds and lower heating costs. Visit The National Arbor Day Foundation website (www.ArborDay.org) for lots of information and free resources. If you live in the city, challenge your city to celebrate Arbor Day and become a Tree City USA. All the information you need is on the Arbor Day website.

BIODIESEL BUSES

Encourage your school district to use biodiesel in your school buses. Biodiesel is a less polluting alternative fuel and is available in all 50 states. Do some homework on the Biodiesel website (www.biodiesel.org) so you can present the facts to your school district. There is a guide for buying biodiesel (www.biodiesel.org/buyingbiodiesel/guide/default.shtm) that is very helpful. There's even a map with cities where you can purchase it.

DAY 96 *It is better to take many small steps in the right direction than to make a great leap forward only to stumble backward. ~ Louis Saschar*

DAY 99 *In my experience, nothing worthwhile has ever really been all that easy. But it certainly has been worthwhile regardless how difficult it seemed.*

Mary Lou Retton has a list of accomplishments that is impressive no matter who you are.

She is...

- The 1st American woman to win gold in gymnastics in the Olympics
- The 1st and only American ever (including today) to win the Olympic All Around Title
- The first female to appear on a Wheaties® cereal box as well as the first female spokesperson for Wheaties® plus scores of other achievements.

As extraordinary as all that is, it is encouraging to note that Mary Lou is not perfect. Her gymnastics scores were often times a "perfect 10." As a teen, this petite powerhouse awed the multitudes in each of these sporting events: Uneven Bars, Vault, Team and Floor Exercise.

Yet as a baby she was born with a hip condition called hip dysplasia that required a hip replacement. Not only that, but she has suffered with both an overactive bladder and arthritis. As part of her public persona as a sports celebrity, she admitted her problems and gave her support to the medications that combat these conditions.

Mary Lou battled competitors on the mat and her body off the mat. A severe wrist injury and knee surgery forced her to decide whether to quit her beloved gymnastics or try to overcome the injuries.

Sitting on the sidelines was not where this dynamo wanted to be. She

worked hard. She exercised. She did the strength training exercises. She sweated. She cried. But she did not give up. She kept on and on until one day she was back. She could participate again in the sport she loved and that loved her back.

Mary Lou went on to be inducted into both the National Italian American Sports Hall of Fame and the International Gymnastics Hall of Fame.

As an engaging public speaker Mary Lou tells audiences *"to never give up on your dreams! Work hard!"* She knows what it is to feel the applause of millions world-wide, and she knows the solitary agony of pain and rehabilitation.

I want to encourage you to think about your life story. How do you want it to read? You may not want to compete for the gold and hear the applause of millions. But even if your goal is more common than Mary Lou's - keep at it until you get it. Never give up. Refresh your determination and revise your target. You can do it!

DAY 101   *Life isn't as magical here, and you're not the only one who feels like you don't belong, or that it's better somewhere else. But there ARE things worth living for. And the best part is you never know what's going to happen next.*
        ~O.R. Melling

The key of persistence opens all doors closed by resistance.

START A LOCAL POLICE/URBAN YOUTH RELATIONS TASK FORCE

If your community doesn't already have a Youth Relations Task Force, approach your Police Department to start one. Explore the different ways youth and police can interact in a positive way to make changes in your neighborhood or community.

The idea is to have youth and police officers interact one-on-one to help break down stereotypes each has of the other. And as all of them get to know each other and learn to appreciate and respect each other, that relationship needs to be made public so others learn that police and youth are not enemies but actually want the same things: safe neighborhoods, the desire to help others, etc.

Have a youth vs. police softball (volleyball, etc.) game and publicize it. Afterward have everyone who played opposite each other give little talks about cooperation, respect, etc. to those who watched.

The youth can join officers on their rounds. This will, of course, take some training prior to actually going out. Sometimes they'll have to stay in the squad car – depending on the kind of call. Other times they might actually walk the streets with the officers.

Do whatever it takes to make relationships between youth and police a positive and constructive one in your neighborhood.

BECOME A COUNSELOR FOR A TELEPHONE HOTLINE.

So many times kids just need someone to talk to who cares. Training is available and people are nearby to help with calls that you can't handle. Kids who are hurting sometimes just need to talk to someone who cares – that can be you!

MARTIAL ARTS INSTRUCTOR

Do you know Yoga, Tai Chi or Karate? Why not teach a free class at your local YMCA or community center? There are lots of individuals (kids and adults) who would enjoy such a class but can't afford to pay. Help people get in shape, give back to your community, and make some friends all at the same time!

DAY 105 *Do not sit still; start moving now. In the beginning, you may not go in the direction you want, but as long as you are moving, you are creating alternatives and possibilities. ~ Rodolfo Costa*

DAY 106   *There is no such thing as helplessness. It's just another word for giving up.*

"Come on ma'am... time to move on."

Kimball peeked at the park worker through sleepy eyes. The morning songbirds serenaded her as she gathered her bags. The singer drew in a deep cleansing breath and glanced at her watch... only an hour until her shift started at Grady Memorial Hospital in Atlanta, Georgia. Kimball was a respected volunteer. She was also homeless. Her home that day was a park in downtown Atlanta.

Kimball believed there were people less fortunate than herself – and they were the patients in the hospital. Every day she gave of her time, her heart and her song to help those recuperating from surgery, accidents and disease.

An accomplished singer and orator, Kimball had not always been homeless.

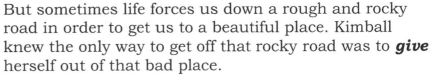

But sometimes life forces us down a rough and rocky road in order to get us to a beautiful place. Kimball knew the only way to get off that rocky road was to **give** herself out of that bad place.

So, Kimball William's literally sang and volunteered her way onto a smoother road. She became an advocate for the poor, abused and destitute; as she took care of so many others, local leaders noticed and took care of her. She had left the rocky pathway and found herself on the way to a more successful life again.

Kimball never forgets where she has been. She is known throughout Georgia for her outlandish but gorgeous hair bows, her generosity and her voice. She is not a part time volunteer. She does not work on others' behalf in her spare time. Now that she has a home and a career as a sought after singer and speaker, she still devotes her time to several causes and events.

She has become the voice of *"Feed The People Christmas Party,"* a Christmas party for homeless, abandoned, abused and generally underprivileged children. Kimball is also involved in a long list of fundraisers. She knows only too well that poverty, abuse and disease never rest and so neither does she.

As I read over her life, I was amazed at this beautiful woman. Sometimes you read of someone you'd like to meet and take to dinner, and for me, Kimball is one such lady. Undaunted in her life's passion and mission to serve others, she let nothing stop her. Not even being homeless. I am in awe of her strength and tenacity to keep on like she did. And I'm sure there were times she wanted to give up and quit. But she didn't.

You have the same choice every single day. No matter what your circumstances are; you can choose to quit or you can choose to press through.

It's up to you.

DAY 107 *Do it badly; do it slowly; do it fearfully; do it any way you have to do it, but DO IT. ~ Steve Chandler*

DAY 108   *It may take a little time to get where you want to be, but if you pause and think for a moment, you will notice you are no longer where you were. Do not stop – keep going.*

DAY 109   *The Motto of Champions: If you are hurt, you can suck it up and press on. If injured, you can rebound and return bigger and better... and continue to inspire. ~ T.F. Hodge*

THEATER ANYONE??

Do you enjoy going to the theater (live performances)? Volunteer to help and you'll get to see the shows for free. Volunteers usually greet the people, take tickets, hand out programs, help with refreshments at intermissions, and provide information. Involve your family or friends, and have a fun, free evening!

WINDOW DRESSING

Have you ever thought of doing "window dressing"? You know - when you walk by a store and look at their window displays? Volunteer at a nonprofit thrift store to do their window displays and floor displays.

PAINT ANGELS

Get a group of friends together and paint houses over the holidays or during the summer. There are many people who simply cannot afford to pay for professional painters and would be thrilled to have some caring youth do it for them. Contact your place of worship, or a volunteer center in your area. They will be thrilled you want to help!

ZOO TIME

Organize a trip for low-income kids to the local zoo or park. Some kids never get out of their neighborhoods because their parents are working 2 and 3 jobs and just don't have the time to take them. Contact an emergency shelter, community center or your place of worship for help locating and organizing the trip. Get parents to drive and accompany you. Be sure to get permission slips signed by the children's parents. The organization you're working with will have one you can use.

DAY 110   *P is for Persistence. Nothing in the world can take the place of persistence. Wishing will not; talent will not; genius will not; education will not. Persistence is like a Genie that creates a magical force in your life.*

_____
_____
_____
_____
_____
_____
_____
_____
_____
_____
_____
_____
_____
_____
_____
_____
_____
_____
_____
_____
_____
_____
_____
_____
_____
_____
_____
_____

DAY 112 *To ask, "How do you do it?" is already starting off on the wrong foot. When reaching for the stars, there does not have to be a 'How' if there is a big enough WHY.*

DAY 113 *It is a noble responsibility to not back down when you know that you know that you know that you are right.*

Have you ever had someone comment on something you said or did, and you responded with, "that's just how I am"? Perhaps it was something astute that you said, a keen observation that you made, or something you did that they thought was extraordinary, but to you it wasn't especially impressive.

Let's see what Jane's story can reveal to you today...

Jane was born in 1934 in London, England and grew up on the southern coast of England. As long as she can remember, she'd loved animals.

When Jane was two years old, her father gave her a life-like toy chimpanzee named Jubilee. Well-meaning friends warned him that it would frighten her, but she adored the toy. (In fact, she still has it and it currently sits on a chair in her home in England.)

At age four, Jane stayed on a farm and helped collect hen's eggs. When she asked the adults how the hens could lay such big eggs, no one answered to her satisfaction. So she hid in the small, stuffy hen house for four hours to find out! (If you've ever been around young children this age, you know that's pretty extraordinary. Actually, it would be amazing for any age kid, and many adults!)

Unknown to Jane, the family had called the police; everyone was frantically trying to locate the missing four-year-old. Imagine her family's relief and amazement, when Jane came rushing out of the hen house in great excitement to tell them how hens lay eggs. Instead of scolding her youngster, Jane's mother sat down with her and listened intently.

Not surprisingly, Jane's favorite childhood books included *The Story of Dr. Dolittle, The Jungle Book,* and the Tarzan books. By age 10 or 11, she was dreaming of going to Africa to live with animals. But instead of discouraging her, Jane's mother said, *"Jane, if you really want something, and if you work hard, take advantage of the opportunities, and never give up, you will somehow find a way."*

Believing her mother's words, Jane did what it took to get to Africa and at age 23 finally sailed to Kenya. While there she heard of a famous paleontologist and anthropologist by the name of Dr. Louis Leakey. She got an appointment to meet him and ended up being interviewed by him about Africa and its wildlife. Dr. Leakey hired her as his assistant, and together with Mrs. Leakey,

they traveled to Olduvai Gorge on a fossil-hunting expedition.

After three months at Olduvai Gorge, the group returned to Nairobi, Kenya and Jane worked at the museum there. Soon after, Jane and Dr. Leakey spoke about Jane studying a group of chimpanzees on the shores of Lake Tanganyika.

"I could have gone on at the museum," Jane said. *"Or I could have learned a lot more about fossils and become a paleontologist. But both these careers had to do with dead animals. And I still wanted to work with living animals.*

My childhood dream was as strong as ever.

Somehow I must find a way to watch free, wild animals living their own undisturbed lives. I wanted to learn things that no one else knew, uncover secrets through patient observation. I wanted to come as close to talking to animals as I could."

At first the British authorities resisted the idea of a young woman living among wild animals in Africa. But they finally agreed to Leakey's proposal when Jane's mother volunteered to accompany her for the first three months. In 1960, Jane and her mother arrived at Gombe National Park in Tanganyika (now Tanzania).

And the rest is history...

Jane Goodall's years of solitary, patient observation and research taught us that chimps hunt for meat, use tools and have unique personalities. Her "few month field study" turned into the longest such study of any animal species in their natural surroundings.

Jane writes: *"The most wonderful thing about fieldwork, whether with chimps, baboons or any other wildlife, is waking up and asking yourself, 'What am I going to see today?' ...It can be exhausting - climbing high, far and fast.*

Around 3 pm you feel very weary because of spending a lot of the day on your tummy, crawling, with vines catching your hair. Living under the skies, the forest is for me a temple, a cathedral made of tree canopies and dancing light, especially when it's raining and quiet. That's heaven on earth for me. I can't imagine going through life without being tuned into the mystical side of nature. People are too busy nowadays."

You see, Jane wasn't doing anything extraordinary on purpose – she was simply fulfilling her purpose – her childhood dream of living with and observing animals. She was living out the proclamation: that's just how I am.

Though you're not an adult yet, the odds are that life has knocked your dream out of you... Do you remember your childhood dream – what you answered when someone asked you what you wanted to do "when you grew up"?

Does it still make your heart race? Can you still see yourself living it out? If your answers are "yes," you've most likely just identified your passion – your life's purpose. And it's never too late to reclaim it!

Believe Jane's mother's words: *"...if you really want something, and if you work hard, take advantage of the opportunities, and never give up, you will somehow find a way."*

Jane did – and so can you!

DAY 114 *If you can't figure out your purpose, figure out your passion. For your passion will lead you right into your purpose.*

DAY 115   *It doesn't interest me what you want to do for a living. I want to know what you ache for, and if you dream of meeting your heart's longing. ~Oriah*

DAY 116   *You can't connect the dots looking forward; you can only connect them looking backwards. So you have to trust that the dots will somehow connect in your future. You have to trust in something – your guy, destiny, life, karma, whatever. This approach has never let me down, and it has made all the difference in my life.* ~ Steve Jobs

BIRD FEEDERS

Birds are always a delight for those who are housebound to watch. Take over a bird feeder (or two) and keep it filled with bird seed. What joy it will bring!

You could even take them a bird identification book and some binoculars. Your gift can turn long boring days into days of fun and discovery.

HOLIDAY DECORATOR

The elderly and homebound often miss out on the fun of holidays because they aren't able to handle the traditions and decorations, yet they usually have boxes of items that made their holidays special over the years. Go over, pull out those boxes and help them decorate – then make sure you go back to put them all away! And if they're going to be alone, invite them to join you for dinner!

PARTY WITH A TWIST!

Do you like to throw parties? Throw a big party and invite as many people as you can fit. Their "ticket" to the event will be a bag full of groceries for the local food pantry. Make sure to send along a list of what the Food Pantry needs most.

You could also pick a favorite charity, and then ask people to bring a donation in lieu of a gift. Announce the total at the party and then send information about the charity to everyone who came so they can feel more a part of it.

AMNESTY INTERNATIONAL

Contact Amnesty International and start writing letters to prisoners in foreign countries. Whether it's just you, your class, or your fellow employees – you will make a huge difference to those receiving the letters.

DAY 117   *The heart of human excellence often begins to beat when you discover a pursuit that absorbs you, frees you, challenges you, or gives you a sense of meaning, joy, or passion. ~ Terry Orlick*

DAY 118 *There is no greater gift you can give or receive than to honor your calling. It's why you were born. And how you become most truly alive. ~ Oprah Winfrey*

DAY 119 *We're the creators of our own experience – remembering this, and living our lives from this perspective, empowers us. ~ Mike Robbins*

DAY 120 *If your life is cloudy and you're far, far off course, you may have to go on faith for a while, but eventually you'll learn that every time you trust your internal navigation system, you end up closer to your right life.* ~ Martha Beck

His parents were too busy running their tavern and basically ignored their son. To cover his unhappiness, George took advantage of every opportunity to cause trouble. He stole, skipped school, chewed tobacco, and drank whiskey – all before he was 7 years old.

It was the police who finally got the parents to pay attention to their son. Their response to the problem was to place their son in a reformatory-orphanage. They rarely saw him again. George, unable to adapt to the strict regulations of St. Mary's Industrial School for boys, was quickly classified as

incorrigible. It was probably the nicest thing they could say.

Until... one man saw promise within the boy and introduced him to the game of baseball.

Whether you're a baseball fan or not – everyone knows the name Babe Ruth. The very name draws up the image of homeruns.

When you learn more about him the name also conjures images of drinking bouts, devoured hot dogs, partying and carousing. Babe Ruth never gave up his wild ways; he simply found a way to channel some of them doing what he loved to do – play baseball.

He actually began his march to fame as a pitcher – setting many records for his prowess on the mound with the Boston Red Sox. His famed pitching, and impressive hitting, wasn't enough though... the Boston Red Sox owner, needing money to finance his dreams of Broadway, sold the Babe to the New York Yankees. It was another in a long line of rejections the Babe had experienced.

He could have let his bitterness stop his life and halt his drive to success and fame. He made a different choice. He kept playing. He kept swinging. He kept doing what he loved. He played baseball.

His ability to hit homeruns exploded. He became famous. He created homerun records that stood for decades. He smiled, laughed, lived life to the fullest – and he kept on swinging.

Here's the thing most people don't talk about. While it's true he hit more homeruns than anyone else; it's also true he struck out more times than anyone. He only hit a homerun, on average, every 11 times at bat. He failed more times than he succeeded. Did you get that?

He failed more times than he succeeded!

Yet he went on to become an American icon; loved by millions; a household name.

Why? Because he chose to keep swinging! A strike out. A walk. A single. They were all necessary to get him to the next homerun. He kept swinging.

As I have studied the lives of successful people I have seen this truth. Most have failed more times than they have succeeded. Yet they choose to keep swinging until they finally connect with the right thing: the right business; the right relationship; the right way to do something. They learn from every failure and jump right back into the game.

Have you failed at something? More than one *something*? Great! Stay in the game. Keep swinging. You'll finally connect. You'll find that right thing; you'll meet that right person; you'll discover the right way. The only way you can fail is if you put the bat down and choose to stop swinging

DAY 121 *You can't just sit there and wait for people to give you that golden dream, you've got to get out there and make it happen for yourself.* ~ *Diana Ross*

DAY 122 *Notice when your heart leaps up in joyous exuberance... In these moments the voice of your spirit is speaking directly to you. ~ Justine Willis Toms*

DAY 123 *If you prepare yourself at every point as well as you can...you will be able to grasp opportunity for broader experience when it appears. ~ Eleanor Roosevelt*

USED SPORTS EQUIPMENT

If your child plays a sport, talk to all their teammates and have them bring in their old equipment. Much of it will still be in great shape. Have the kids donate it to a team in a less fortunate part of town, or find a group overseas that will be thrilled to receive the equipment for teams in their own country that have nothing.

One young soccer player in the United States not only gathered equipment from all her teammates – she contacted every team in the area. What she collected was enough to provide equipment for the children in 20 African villages. Wow!

LAKE ANGEL

If you live on a lake, do your part in keeping it clean. Go out in your boat and pick up trash and debris in the lake. Recycle what you can and dispose of the rest. Let your friends and community know. They will be inspired by your actions and be eager to help.

MINI- NURSERY

Start your own mini-nursery to beautify areas in your community. Most shrubs can be rooted from a cutting. Ask your local nursery for extra pots, or let your community know you need them (you'll get plenty!). Buy some rooting compound, dip the cuttings, and plant them in your pots full of potting soil. Don't be afraid to ask an expert for their help. When your new plants are established plant them all over town or in people's yards. It won't cost you anything but the rewards will be huge.

ANNUAL SEEDING TRAYS

In keeping with the idea above, start your own "Annual Seeding Trays" when it is the right time in your area. Many people can't afford to buy plants from the nursery. You can start them yourself from seed, and then give them to people in your community. You can create so much beauty with so little money. When local merchants realize what you're doing they may even donate the soil and seeds – especially if you promote them when you give the plants away.

181

POWERFUL WOMAN PLEDGE

I raise my hand to be a POWERFUL WOMAN.

I will take time TODAY to make a difference in the world.

I will take time TODAY to do one thing – for one person.

I will take time TODAY to spread some love & caring in my world.

One thing – TODAY.

EVERYDAY!

Nothing is too small. Nothing is too big.

It is only important to take Action.

I will take time TODAY – to ACT – to create CHANGE!

Realize deeply that the present moment is all you ever have.
~ Eckhart Tolle

From Pennies to Millions

Marion Luna Brem was 30 years old when she was handed a death sentence. Marion had cancer of the breast and cervix. In the short span of eleven weeks, she had two surgeries: a mastectomy and hysterectomy. Next she suffered through the horrible effects of chemotherapy.

In addition to her pain, the cancer had robbed her of her hair, her savings and her husband. He left because he couldn't deal with the pressure any more. He left Marion with two small boys and no way to support them.

One hot morning Marion found herself on the floor of her bathroom trying not to throw up again. She was not only facing overwhelming pain and paralyzing fear; she was facing a major decision. Would she give up and choose death, or would she fight back? Thoughts of her children consumed her – making her realize she had to choose to live for them.

She needed to get a job, but she had little work experience and next to no formal education. Add to that equation the fact she was a woman - and a Latina, and the prospects looked as dismal as the bathroom floor.

Marion's best friend suggested a job in sales. At first Marion pushed the idea aside. And then she decided to act on it. She chose the male dominated car sales industry. In her healthier days she'd been a switchboard operator at a car dealership and knew there was good money in car sales. She'd also witnessed how the salesmen talked exclusively to the men and virtually ignored the women.

Her instincts told her women were a more important part of the equation than they were given credit for. Statistics now prove she was right. When couples buy a car, the woman influences the decision 80% of the time.

It wasn't an easy road. Marion was flatly refused applications (because she was a woman) in 16 car dealerships. Finally, at the 17th car dealership she told the manager what she'd observed about women car buyers. He hired her on the spot.

Her all-male colleagues welcomed the rookie. They didn't see her as competition, but rather as a curiosity. It wasn't until she started outperforming them that they became cool toward her. Even so, Marion received the annual "Salesman of the Year" award -- complete with a man's Rolex watch. She accepted the recognition and enjoyed her achievement.

Marion was the top producer for the next two years. Then she approached her boss for a management position. He refused her because he didn't want to remove her from sales -- she was making too much money for the company.

Difficult as it was, Marion left the security of that position and hit the pavement again. She was finally hired as an entry-level manager at a new dealership. Two and half years later she was ready to start her own dealership.

She went to the drugstore and bought 50 school folders and created portfolios. She called them her "brag folder" and they contained her certificates, press clippings and a biography. She sent the package to 50 CPAs all over Texas. Two weeks later she received a call from one of her contacts. He became her silent partner, put up the working capital and millions in loans, and Marion opened a Chrysler dealership.

Just 5 years after selling her first car, Marion Luna Brem opened "Love Chrysler", complete with a heart logo on every car. Marion's motto: *"It's not just the hearts on our cars, it's the hearts inside our people. We're spreading Love all over Texas!"*

Today Marion is cancer-free, the owner of two car dealerships, and recently celebrated the 11th anniversary of Love Chrysler. Her company is 89th on the Hispanic Business 500 with revenues of more than $45 million.

Success is a frame of mind that takes action. Believe in yourself. Keep moving forward. And remember Marion! Hopefully your journey does not begin as tragically as Marion's but use her determination and belief to keep going!

DAY 129 *Keep away from people who try to belittle your ambitions. Small people always do that, but the really great make you feel that you, too, can become great.* ~ *Mark Twain*

_____

_____

_____

_____

_____

_____

_____

_____

_____

_____

_____

_____

_____

_____

_____

_____

_____

_____

_____

_____

_____

_____

_____

_____

_____

DAY 130 *Do not go where the path may lead; go instead where there is no path and leave a trail. ~ Ralph Waldo Emerson*

PLASTIC BAGS

In many areas you can't recycle plastic bags with your regular recycling. Go around your neighborhood once a month to collect the plastic bags, then take them to a local grocery store that recycles them.

COMPOSTING

Start a compost pile in your neighborhood, and then use it to provide rich soil for a garden that will create food for the hungry in your community. Think how much food and gardening/yard waste can be composted to make a difference!

DISCARDED COMPUTERS

Are you good with computers and fixing things? How about taking discarded computer parts and creating "new" machines that you can give away to people who need them?

SPECIAL PERSON BOOK

Is there someone in your community or family that is well-known and loved? Do a special project to let them know...

1) Put together a list of questions:
- When, where and why did you get to know this person?
- What famous person do they remind you of?
- What are your favorite memories of this person?
2) Ask for any pictures or mementos they have
3) Send a copy to as many people who know this person as possible.
4) Gather everything and bind them in a book.

Your gift will be a treasure for the rest of their lives!

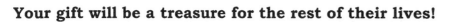

DAY 131 *It is not because things are difficult that we do not dare; it is because we do not dare that they are difficult. ~ Seneca*

DAY 132 *Pay no attention to what the critics say; no statue has ever been erected to a critic.*

DAY 133   *Those who try to do something and fail are infinitely better than those who try to do nothing and succeed.* ~ *Lloyd Jones*

Jean's background certainly didn't indicate tremendous success for the future. Born in New York, she graduated from high school with a partial college scholarship but couldn't attend because her family couldn't pay the rest. She decided to attend a business school but had barely begun when her father died – forcing her to quit and take a fulltime job.

She moved from one low paying job to another, eventually marrying and becoming a homemaker and mother of two. She left the work place, but devoted a lot of time to working with various organizations and charities.

And she kept gaining weight. She had been overweight as a child. She was

overweight as an adult. She tried everything to conquer her problem – diets, doctors, medications. Nothing worked long-term.

She was desperate to find a way to conquer her problem so she headed for the New York Health Obesity Clinic. She was given a diet to follow but she fell right back into the cheating that always defeated her. She kept her failures to herself. The woman running the clinic had never been overweight. *"How could she understand the cheating of an overweight housewife?"* Jean asked.

Desperate for someone to talk to, she invited 6 overweight friends to her house. The first meeting was so helpful they decided to meet weekly to share their successes and struggles.

The meeting kept growing as more women joined them. Soon she was organizing meetings for hundreds of women – charging just 25 cents a week to cover costs. Her weight kept coming off. When she reached her personal goal she reached out to help her family. Her husband lost 70 pounds. Her mother shed 57. From her victory, and the victories of those she reached out to help, she began to realize this was bigger than just her original desire to lose weight.

On May 15, 1963, Weight Watchers was born.

From the living room of her small New York home, Weight Watchers grew to an international business worth millions - that **helped** millions. Jean Nidetch remained slim and became the spokeswoman for her exploding company, traveling all around the world – helping others change their lives the same way she did.

Her Success Secret? She found a way to solve a problem of her own, and then invited other people along on the journey.

Weight Watchers®

I've had people tell me, *"Ginny, all the problems have been solved, and all the ideas for making money have been used."*

Hogwash! As long as there is life there will be problems. There will be ideas for success. Your job is to get out of your tiny little "box" and start thinking and dreaming of solutions. Her other Success Secret?

She never started out to become a millionaire. She started out to solve her own problem. Then she wanted to help others. (Remember, she only charged 25 cents per meeting in the beginning.) Her great success sprang from a desire to make a difference.

Think outside the box. If you want to experience great success in life, start paying attention and see where you can make a difference. It's there. You just have to open your heart and mind to find it. The answer will probably surprise you, but that's half the fun.

DAY 135 *The world has the habit of making room for the person whose words and actions show they know where they are going. ~ Napoleon Hill*

DAY 136 *The greater danger for most of us is not that our aim is too high and we miss it, but that it is too low and we reach it. ~ Michelangelo*

DAY 137   *Your life is in your hands, to make of it what you choose.*
              ~ John Kehoe

_____

_____

_____

_____

_____

_____

_____

_____

_____

_____

_____

_____

_____

_____

_____

_____

_____

_____

_____

_____

_____

_____

_____

_____

_____

_____

_____

BIRTHDAY PLEDGE CAMPAIGN

Let's say you're 29 years old (put whatever age you are in the equation!) Start your own "30 – 4 – 30 Campaign" when you turn 30 years old.

Instead of just claiming gifts, walk one mile for each of your 30 years and ask friends to pledge money in lieu of a birthday gift. Then send your money to a cause dear to you.

If you're not a walker it could be biking 30 miles, swimming 30 laps, writing 30 letters to soldiers – whatever your interest is... turn it into a way to make a difference!
Your birthday will mean so much more!

GROCERIES FOR THE HOMELESS

Give Grocery Gift Certificates to the Homeless in your area. Talk to your local grocery store and have them create Gift Certificates that exclude alcohol. Then hand them out to Homeless people asking for help.

CREATE A "BIRTHDAY JAR" OR A "YOU'RE SPECIAL JAR"

Too often it's easy to notice the things we DON'T like about people – the things that irritate us. How about taking the time to come up with all the reasons we are THANKFUL for the people in our lives?
Here are some ideas:
- You fix the best lunches
- You make sure I leave in the morning with a smile
- You always have a smile for people
- You keep in shape

Come up with as many as you can – trying for 365 if it's a Birthday Jar – but any amount will make a difference to the person receiving it. Print out the whole list, cut out each entry, and put them in a big jar. Whether you use an old mayonnaise jar or a beautiful ceramic one, it's what inside that will change the world for the person receiving it.

DAY 138 *Let others lead small lives, but not you. Let others argue over small things, but not you. Let others cry over small hurts, but not you. Let others leave their future in someone else's hands, but not you. ~ Jim Rohn*

DAY 139 *Make your life a masterpiece. Join the ranks of those people who live what they teach, who walk their talk.*

DAY 141 *For true success ask yourself these 4 questions: Why? Why not? Why not me? Why not now? ~ James Allen*

Debbi was only 19 years old when she reached a cross-road in her life. She was married to a well-known Economist and Futurist, and had quit work to play the role of a conventional wife. She hadn't expected her decision to deal such a hard blow to her self-esteem. No one seemed to think she had anything to offer – including herself.

One night, at a party, things reached a head. People were falling all over themselves to talk to her husband – they were treating *her* like she was an absolute zero, walking away from her in most conversations. Until the party host approached her... She *tried* to talk to him; answering his barrage of questions. She *tried* to appear sophisticated, urbane and clever – failing miserably at her attempt to be something she wasn't.

Her host finally asked, "What do you intend to *do* with your life?"

Debbi was a nervous wreck at this point. She blurted out, "Well, I'm mostly trying to get orientated."

Her host looked at her with disgust. "The word is oriented," he snapped. "There is no such word as *orientated*. Why don't you learn to use the English language?" He spat out his words and walked away.

Well, you can imagine. . . Debbi was crushed. She cried all the way home. But somewhere, in the middle of all the tears, she made a decision. She would never, never, NEVER let something like that happen again. She was done living in someone else's shadow. She would find something of her own.

As she pondered what she was going to do she thought back to the old boat motor that had accumulated dust in her family's basement when she was growing up – her parents and 5 girls in a 2-bedroom, 1 bathroom home. Her father was going to buy a boat for that motor *someday*. He never did, and to Debbi that motor became a symbol of putting off dreams until it's too late to achieve them.

Debbi had watched her father die with his dreams unfulfilled. She didn't want the same thing to happen to her. She would do *something.*

But what?!

The only thing Debbi was really good at was making cookies. She had been baking and experimenting with recipes since was

13. She'd add more butter; use less flour; or try different kinds of chocolate. She'd finally hit on a recipe that she believed was ideal. Her cookies were soft, buttery and crammed with chocolate chips.

She realized she had to use her gifts so. . . Debbi decided to open a cookie store. Every single person in her life told her it wouldn't work. No one believed in her.

It didn't matter. On August 18, 1977, when Debbi was 20, she opened her first store. No one came. By noon she was desperate. She stared at the empty store and decided if she was going to go out of business, she would at least do it in style.

Debbi loaded up a tray of cookies and went out in to her shopping arcade, trying to give away cookies. No one would take them. She figured she had nothing to lose at this point, so she headed out to the street. She begged, pleaded and wheedled until people finally took her samples. She smiled as their faces lit up.

She went back to the store and sold cookies to the people who had followed her wanting more. By the end of the day she had sold $50 worth. The next day she sold $75 worth.

The rest is Cookie History. . .

Debbi Fields went on to own over 600 stores – with sales in the multi-millions. She is also the mother of 5. She did indeed find something of her own!

You will face obstacles. You will face people who don't believe in your dreams. So what? It's YOUR life. It will become what YOU decide to make it.

Debbi Fields shared this in a speech she gave: **"Whatever you do in your life, you have to be absolutely passionate about it."**

Debbi was passionate about cookies. Passionate about excellence. Passionate about living with no regrets.

Take some time to think about what you are passionate about. Make a list. It might be long. It might be short. What are you MOST passionate about? What will create the greatest joy and success in your life if you decide to do it? What will you most regret if you *don't* do it?

Right now – TODAY – you have gifts that can make a difference in how you live your life. How will you use them? What will you do? It's up to you, and I know whatever you decide, you will be successful!

DAY 142 *Issue a blanket pardon. Forgive everyone who has ever hurt you in any way. Forgiveness is a perfectly selfish act. It sets you free from the past. ~ Brian Tracy*

DAY 143   *Our greatest glory is not in never failing, but in rising up every time we fail. ~ Ralph Waldo Emerson*

DAY 144   *Learn to enjoy every minute of your life. Be happy NOW. Don't wait for something outside of yourself to make you happen.*

INSTRUMENT DRIVE

Put a notice in your local paper or get your local radio to help you with an "Instrument Drive". Trust me; there are a lot of musical instruments lying around in people's homes that can make a huge difference for kids and people of all ages. You'll give someone a chance to create music, as well as breathe new life into old instruments that are simply collecting dust.

TURBANS

Make turbans for women undergoing chemotherapy who have lost their hair. If you like to sew, or are willing to learn something simple to help others, this is for you. Visit the following webpage for a simple pattern and easy to follow instructions: http://www.sewing.org/enthusiast/html/ec_turban.html

MAKE A CHILD SMILE

Go to http://www.MakeAChildSmile.org This wonderful organization features three new children each month that are fighting illness. They tell you about the child, then list a PO box you can send a card or small gift to. They'll also send updates as the parents send them in. For the price of a card and a stamp you can make a huge difference to a child fighting for their life!

LOCKS OF LOVE

Locks of Love is a wonderful way you can make a difference if you have long hair, or if you are willing to grow your hair. Go to http://www.locksoflove.org. This amazing organization provides prosthetic hair pieces to kids 18 years old and younger who have long term hair loss due to a medical condition. Most of the children helped by Locks of Love have lost their hair due to a medical condition called alopecia areata, which has no known cause or cure. The prostheses they provide help to restore their self-esteem and their confidence, enabling them to face the world and their peers. Visit their website to find out what a huge difference your hair can make!

Then collect a group of your friends who are willing to join you. Have a big celebration the day you all go to donate your hair!

We are what we repeatedly do. Excellence, then, is not an act, but a habit

~ Aristotle

_____

_____

_____

_____

_____

_____

_____

_____

_____

_____

_____

_____

_____

_____

_____

_____

_____

_____

_____

_____

_____

_____

_____

_____

_____

Impossible is a word to be found only in the dictionary of fools.
~ Napoleon Bonaparte

DAY 147 *Twenty years from now you will be more disappointed by the things you did not do than by the ones you did do. So throw off the bowlines. Sail away from the safe harbor. Catch the trade winds in your sails. Explore. Dream. Discover.*

Many years ago a movement swept through America. The call went out to all who had the courage and vision to "Head West." What a picture was drawn for them. . . *The West is where you want to be. There is land for everyone - for the taking! Beautiful. Fertile. Opportunity for everyone. Don't miss your opportunity to be one of the first to stake your claim!*

The call went out and hordes signed up to join the wagon trains pulling out of Independence, Missouri. As the pioneers bought supplies and lined up their wagons, their eyes shone with the excitement of what would be waiting at the end of the trail. I think it fair to say not one of them had a real understanding of what lay between Missouri and the far west they envisioned in their dreams.

Can't you hear the conversation. . .?

"Why, honey," one confident husband says to his rather nervous wife, *"there isn't going to be anything to this. We've got a nice, sturdy wagon. We're all together, and we have plenty of food. We're just going to roll along the trail for a while and soon we'll have everything we've dreamed of. Just think of it!"*

I don't know how long before the starry looks faded from their eyes - somewhere between broken wagon wheels and Indian attacks. Maybe it was the weevils in the flour, or the snowstorm that left them stranded in the mountains for months on end. Perhaps it was losing a child to illness because there were not enough medical supplies, or simply the fatigue that came from fighting the dust, heat, and long days of the grueling cruelness of the trail.

Every pioneer who started down the trail, if they didn't die, had one of three things happen. Some gave up and turned back. Others decided they couldn't take any more and simply built a house where they stopped. Then there were the others... the ones who made it all the way to the West.

Yes, somewhere along the way the starry look faded from their eyes. . . *faded.* . . to be replaced by determination. Broken wagon wheels, Indian attacks, weevils, snowstorms, death, fatigue, choking dust, and long days... They all became daily obstacles to be endured and overcome, but at some point each person who made it, simply decided nothing was going to stop them. They had left behind their former lives to go someplace new. **They were going...**

So what about you? Do you have a dream? Do you have something you've started, but then turned back because it seemed too hard? Or maybe you're still on the trail, wondering which obstacle will be the one to destroy what you've worked so hard for.

Maybe you're just looking at the trail, thinking, *"No way. Not me. That just looks too hard."* Yet your heart yearns to go where the trail will take you.

You have a choice to make every single day. You can stay right where you are, or you can go on an adventure to accomplish what you dream of accomplishing. Not going may seem safer, but the truth is that not going will only assure you stay right where you are in your life.

What do you want? Where do you want to go? The only way to get there is to start your journey, and then determine to not let anything stop you!

_____

_____

_____

_____

_____

_____

_____

_____

_____

_____

_____

_____

_____

_____

_____

_____

_____

_____

_____

_____

_____

_____

_____

_____

_____

_____

_____

DAY 150 *People become really quite remarkable when they start thinking they can do something. When they believe in themselves they have the first secret of success.*

DAY 151 *What we can or cannot do, what we consider possible or impossible, is rarely a function of our true capability. It is more likely a function of our beliefs about who we are.* ~ Anthony Robbins

POWERFUL WOMAN ACTIONS

SEND A CARD

A REAL card. Not an email. Not an E-card. A real, live, honest-to-God card that you put in the mail with a stamp, or put on someone's pillow, or hide in their locker. There's something about a real card that says how much you love and appreciate someone that is so very special.

Give them something to put on their desk, or stick in a book, or tape to the bathroom mirror as a constant reminder you took the time to do it. Buy one, or make one; they will become treasured gifts. Make a habit of sending at least 1 card a week. You will pour goodness and light into the world!

FAMILY GRATITUDE PARTY

Lead the way in putting together a Family Gratitude Party. Create customized cards or notes thanking some of the people who have made a difference in your lives (grandparents and other relatives, babysitters, teachers, pastors/priests, gardeners, trash collectors, CPAs, doctors, nurses, etc.). Use computer templates, cut out magazine pictures, or let your imagination take over! Help each other with ideas and then mail all the letters at the same time.

FAN THE SPARK CLUB

Your friends may think you've lost it when you suggest this one, but you'll be amazed by the results. Make a list of 5-10 people that you have a hard time loving or respecting – at work, in your neighborhood, at your place of worship...

Now I want you to write a card to each of them – EACH of you putting down something you like about that person. You may have to stretch, but I promise you can do it. You can sign your names, or do it anonymously – it will have the same impact.

Every person has a spark of goodness & greatness in them. They just need to be reminded. You could totally change someone's school experience and life by your willingness to reach out.

If your friends won't join you? So what? Do it yourself and watch your kindness fan sparks all over world!

DAY 152 *All the breaks you need in life wait within your imagination. Imagination is the workshop of your mind, capable of turning mind energy into accomplishment and wealth. ~ Napoleon Hill*

DAY 154 *If you believe in what you are doing, then let nothing hold you up in achieving it. So many of the best accomplishments in the world have been done against seeming impossibilities. ~ Dale Carnegie*

Vicki giggled while the other students in her class pressed their hands over their ears. She found it funny that almost everyone else found the squeak of the chalk on the chalkboard unpleasant. It didn't bother her in the least. In fact, Vicki looked forward to adding her own chalk squeaks to the world of school chalkboards – Vicki knew she was going to be a teacher.

Little did she know where she'd end up teaching and the thousands of lives she would change. . .

Raised in Ripoll, Catalonia (Spain) Vicki had a rapacious appetite for learning. She just couldn't seem to get enough. After graduating from her local university, she taught school for ten years. But then her hunger for learning kicked in again and she attended graduate classes at various universities until she ended up with a Master's Degree from Michigan State University (USA).

Have you ever had a fascination with a place you've heard about but never visited? Well, Vicki did! And her fascination became a deep longing.

There was just something about Nepal and she knew she had to get there. When she arrived in the capital city of Kathmandu in 1988, she was shocked at the poverty and terrible living conditions. After returning home, she couldn't get the images of the street children out of her mind and began thinking about what she could do for these desperate children.

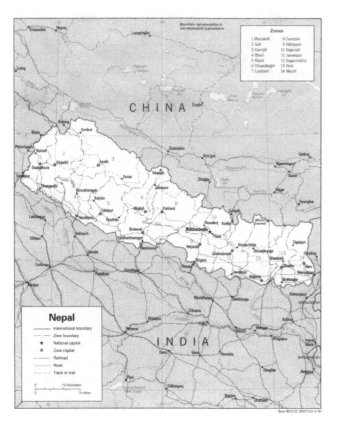

A year later, still haunted by the visions of Kathmandu, Vicki moved to Nepal to learn the country's language and culture first hand. She wound up founding her first of many schools -- Dorgee School which took in 32 refugee children from Tibet. Four years later, steeped in the culture and language of Nepal, she was ready to serve the poorest of the poor – the people that really tugged on her heartstrings. Vicki started the Daleki School in Kathmandu for the most impoverished children, teaching them their culture, history and traditions.

"Teacher, Teacher... there is a girl here... She has nowhere to go." Vicki's heart grew even bigger. . .

A little 7-year-old girl with disabilities was abandoned in a market in Kathmandu and brought to Vicki. In response to yet another need in her adopted country, she opened the Reception Center which provides housing, education and medical attention for special needs children. The classes also prepare the children so they can attend regular schools.

It's not hard to see why the people loved Vicki and turned to her when there was a need. . . Nepal had become part of Vicki even as she had become part of Nepal. . . but it still wasn't enough! Vicki was unstoppable. . . and her huge heart moved her beyond Nepal to Pakistan and Bangladesh where she is setting up schools for the poorest of the poor.

Although Vicki Sherpa has been honored with many awards and her Daleki School is an international model school for poor and marginalized children and adults, her greatest reward is knowing she has made a difference in the lives of thousands of people.

And the key to it all -- she did it by doing what she loves to do – teach.

You see, the secret to success really isn't a secret at all. Harvey Mackay puts it in one simple sentence – *"Find something you love to do and you'll never have to work a day in your life."*

Life is not just about accumulating things, making money or having lots of influence. Life is about fulfilling your purpose. And your purpose is doing what you love to do in a way that helps as many other people as possible.

So don't sell yourself and others short. Take the bold step needed in order to embrace what you love to do.

Make sure that it helps others, and you will truly be leading a powerful life!

DAY 156   *All successful people are big dreamers. They imagine what their future could be, ideal in every respect, and then they work every day toward their distant vision – that goal or purpose.*

DAY 157 *There are no accidents – there is only some purpose that we haven't yet understood. ~Deepak Chopra*

You can because you think you can.

CHEER SOMEONE UP

Start a collection of cartoons, pictures, and anecdotes that make you smile. Whenever you hear of someone who is ill or in need of cheering up, print out an appropriate selection and send it to him or her in a card. So many people in these situations feel forgotten – let them know they aren't!

WAITING LINE ANGEL

When waiting for service where you take a number, trade numbers with someone who has a small child, is physically upset or in a hurry, or is having some kind of difficulty. This simple act of kindness can change the entire atmosphere around you and start a chain-reaction of similar kindnesses.

KINDNESS ZONE

Put up "Kindness Zone" or "Kindness Practiced Here" signs and banners all over your workplace. They are a great way to remind people to think and act with kindness.

RANDOM ACTS OF KINDNESS EVENING

Gather some friends and go out for a "Random Acts of Kindness" evening. Let the situations you find yourselves in dictate the needed kindness. Be spontaneous. Have fun! Enjoy the power of blowing people's minds when you do something just for them!

GLEANING FARM FIELDS

Do you have farmers in your area? In today's world of automated harvesting, there is a lot of crop that gets left behind at the end of the harvest. Contact the farmers and ask if you can "glean" their fields – get all the rest of the crop. Get your friends to help you and then donate all the food to your food bank or to a homeless shelter. ANY kind of food will be appreciated!

DAY 159 *There are those who dream and wish, and there are those who dream and work.*

_____

_____

_____

_____

_____

_____

_____

_____

_____

_____

_____

_____

_____

_____

_____

_____

_____

_____

_____

_____

_____

_____

_____

_____

_____

_____

_____

_____

www.PowerfulWomanStore.com

T-Shirts
Posters
Water Bottles
Mugs
iPhone cases
Jewelry
Notepads
Bags
And so much more...

****

Visit the **POWERFUL WOMAN** Store today!

DAY 161   *Death is not the biggest fear we have; our biggest fear is taking the risk to be alive – the risk to be alive and express what we really are.*

_____

_____

_____

_____

_____

_____

_____

_____

_____

_____

_____

_____

_____

_____

_____

_____

_____

_____

_____

_____

_____

_____

_____

_____

_____

_____

_____

_____

_____

_____

_____

Be miserable. Or motivate yourself. Whatever has to be done, it's

236

HOLOCAUST

"No . . . no . . . help me . . . .Take me out of here . . . .Help. Mama! Daddy! Why?"

Dark and dismal . . . those are the only words to describe the camp. Remembering the lifeless, death-filled days of her childhood in a concentration camp, Trudi promised herself that once that hellacious period of her history came to an end, she would take care of children. Having lost her own childhood to the Nazi's, she passionately pursued giving so other children would have theirs.

Yes, life as a 6 year old during the Holocaust was tragic and horrifying. Yet Trudi defied death numerous times . . . once being literally snatched from the flames of the human incinerator. That unconquerable "life sprit" she possessed spilled over into her every endeavor.

As she grew up, Trudi remembered her promise and after working with immigrants and refugees, she saw her niche.

Her dream? A totally free clinic in Jerusalem that would take care of the children of the poorest of the poor with the best dental care money could buy.

Not content to "put a band aid on a gaping wound," Trudi and husband Zeev require a time commitment from those receiving dental care – from both the children and their families. The kids and their guardians or parents agree to dental education, training and follow up care for months.

Trudi and Zeev truly desire to see their patients better themselves and to feel good about whom they were created to be. In one interview she spoke of "adopting" over 50 kids and 250 families to ensure they all had an education . . . an education that oft times included teaching degrees as well as law, medical and dental schools.

"Ah, vacation at last!" yawned the latest visiting dentist from Norway. *"Can't wait to get started! How many do we have today?"*

"Same as yesterday . . . about 100!" calls out the hygienist with a grin!

Today, the Trudi Birger Dental Clinic is run by the life force of the late Trudi Birger, her devoted husband, Zeev and the organization Dental Volunteers for Israel. The patients are referred through social welfare offices.

Volunteer dentists come to the Clinic from around the world with differing religious backgrounds . . . but with a single passion: to give! They give of their own time, talents and money to come to Israel and treat kids who can't pay them or even say "thank you" in a language the doctors understand. The clinic

treats any child, all children . . . from Jewish to Christian to Muslim . . . any child in need because teeth are teeth!

I want you to understand that while this clinic has the most modern, up to date medical equipment available with some of the best trained doctors and hygienists in the world, *in the beginning days of the clinic, she had nothing . . . no money, resources, no equipment, no*

volunteers . . . nothing except her devoted passion and sweet tempered will. It was solely Trudi's vivacious love of life, her grace and purity of heart that brought every needed resource, from professionals to equipment into reality . . . throughout the years!!!

Trudi loved life and passed that love along to everyone she met, and it was returned to her many, many times over.

WOW! If anyone had a reason to be totally and completely against the world, it was Trudi. Losing her childhood to the horrors of the concentration camps could have tarnished her heart beyond repair. But to read her responses in an interview, is to hear of a very deep and resounding love of people, a belief that all are worthy of respect and passionate joy-filled devotion to life itself.

If that's not a recipe for a powerful life, I don't know what is!

DAY 163   *You can have anything you want, if you want it badly enough. You can be anything you want to be, do anything you set out to accomplish if you hold to that desire with singleness of purpose. ~ Abraham Lincoln*

DAY 164   *If you deliberately plan on being less than you are capable of being, then I warn you that you'll be unhappy for the rest of your life.* ~ *Abraham Maslow*

DAY 165 *Happiness doesn't depend on who you are or what you have; it depends solely upon what you think. ~ Dale Carnegie*

POWERFUL WOMAN ACTIONS

ENLIST YOUR KIDS TO PROVIDE FREE BABYSITTING

Sometimes adults have to take their kids with them to places to talk business because they can't afford a babysitter. Be creative and ask around – maybe a group of your children & their friends, or a club or youth group could offer free babysitting while parents have meetings with teachers. Perhaps a low-cost counseling center could use someone to watch their clients' kids. Maybe a group of your parents' friends would like to go to a movie or out to dinner.

SURPRISE YOUR FRIENDS... OR YOUR ENEMIES!

Give anonymous, surprise gifts to friends, or people you find it difficult to like – with a note telling them they matter. It doesn't have to be much. A candy bar; one cookie; a flower; something you have lying around your house. Every time, it will be the fun of knowing someone cares that will make their life better.

DO YOU LIKE TO READ?

Volunteer at a school or public library to read aloud to children. If the atmosphere lends itself, encourage the children (depending on the number you're reading to) or a few children to act out what you're reading. Use lots of inflection and drama in your reading. Kids just love it! If you have a friend who's an artist, invite him/her to come along and illustrate the story up on an easel while you're reading.

HABITAT FOR HUMANITY

Get a group of your friends together and help at a Habitat for Humanity building project. Sometimes you can help demolish walls, and other times you get to help build them.

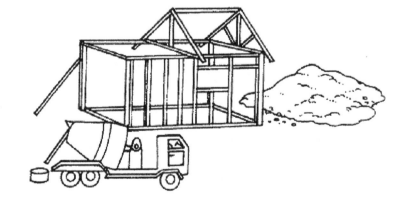

There's a project for everyone no matter what skills you do, or don't have! Go to their website to find a local project in your area (www.habitat.org/cd/local). You'll have a whole lot of fun, maybe learn some new skills, and make some new friends -- all while you're helping someone who couldn't otherwise afford to have a home of their own.

DAY 166 *Self-pity gets you nowhere. One must have the adventurous daring to accept oneself as a bundle of possibilities and undertake the most interesting game in the world – making the most of one's best. ~ Henry Fosdick*

DAY 168 *The nearest way to glory is to strive to be what you wish to be thought to be. ~ Socrates*

_____

_____

_____

_____

_____

_____

_____

_____

_____

_____

_____

_____

_____

_____

_____

_____

_____

_____

_____

_____

_____

_____

_____

_____

_____

_____

_____

_____

_____

_____

DAY 169 *The person who trims herself to suit everybody will soon whittle herself away to nothing.*

"Manya – speak in Russian, not Polish! You might be heard!"

It was hard for little Manya to remember she could speak Polish only at home – never in public. A single conversation in Polish, or even a just a word could bring harm to herself and her family. The year was 1871 and Manya was only 4 years old.

Her country – Poland – had not been an independent country for almost a century. Warsaw was controlled by the Russian czar who tried to stamp out Polish nationalism by keeping the people ignorant of their language and culture. But Polish patriots (like her parents) were determined to not only retain both their culture and their language, but to ultimately regain control of their nation.

Manya's parents were both educators, but were not allowed to teach in certified schools under the repressive czarist regime. Manya was the star pupil in her class and graduated at age 15. Because women were not allowed at the University of Warsaw, Manya and one of her sisters, Bronya, attended an illegal night school dubbed the Floating University. It got its name because the location was changed frequently to help evade the watchful eyes of the authorities.

"Manya...we have to help each other...We need to go to school....You help me through school and then I will help you...we can do it if we work together... Don't you think?"

The two sisters made a pact. Manya would work to put her sister through medical school in Paris. And as soon as she could, Bronya would reciprocate.

During these years, Manya filled her hours with self-taught studies. Not sure what she was really interested in; she studied sociology, literature, physics and chemistry. She discovered that math and the physical sciences were her strength and passion. By the fall of 1891, Manya was able to leave for Paris to begin studies at the University of Paris – the famous Sorbonne.

Manya became Marie when she enrolled at the University. As lonely and difficult as her living situation was, she was able to concentrate on her studies and experienced a liberty and independence she'd never known. Because of her lack of academic preparation she was behind the other students, especially in the physical sciences which the Russians had outlawed in Polish schools. Her proficiency in technical French was also lacking as was her mathematical background – but she loved learning – she was like a sponge. She quickly caught up.

"All that I saw and learned that was new delighted me. It was like a new world opened to me - the world of science - which I was at last permitted to know in all liberty."

Marie's ferocious studying paid off when she finished her master's degree in physics just 2 years later and started her second master's degree in math. But there was a problem. The math degree required lab work and there was no lab available to her at the University.

Her search for lab space resulted in an introduction to another scientist who had done pioneering research on magnetism -- Marie was introduced to

Pierre Curie. This introduction would change not only their individual lives, but also the course of science.

The rest is history . . .

They were married a year later and Pierre, deeply intrigued and respectful of Marie's brilliance, helped her every way he could. (And Marie did the same for Pierre.) Their lives were fraught with deprivation and difficulties due to lack of funding and adequate lab facilities. But both understood the importance of their research and ignored their personal discomfort and pain.

Known best for her discovery of the radioactive elements of polonium and radium, **Marie went on to become the first person to win two Nobel prizes.**

Her radium was a key to the basic change in scientific understanding of energy and matter. And her work not only influenced science, but also began an entirely new era in medical research and treatment.

As a female child growing up in an occupied country, Marie could have come up with all kinds of excuses why she couldn't finish school, go to college, or persevere in her career choice. But she didn't. Marie took the steps necessary to move from one level of life to the next. She faced each obstacle, found a solution and moved forward.

She is a marvelous example of a powerful girl growing into a powerful woman!

DAY 170 *At least 3 times every day take a moment and ask yourself what is really important. Have the wisdom and courage to build your life around your answer. ~ Les Jampolsky*

DAY 171 *To be yourself in a world that is constantly trying to make you something else is the greatest accomplishment. ~ Ralph Waldo Emerson*

DO YOU LOVE OUTDOOR SPORTS?

Do a little research and see if you have an Outdoor Education Center in your area. Often these Centers will help people with special needs and they nearly always need volunteers to help. What could be better than helping someone else experience the joy of skiing or horseback riding, etc.?

HAVE A KIDS COAT DRIVE

Unfortunately there are lots of kids who don't have warm coats for the winter. Call your local elementary schools and ask if they could use coats to give to their students who need them. Then put the word out to neighbors, friends, etc. for clean, "gently used" coat donations (all sizes for elementary kids) and

then donate them to your local elementary schools. If you don't get enough donated, you can go to the local thrift stores and buy some at very low cost (they might also donate them if you tell them what you're doing). Get them cleaned and then deliver them to the schools. There will be some very grateful kids come this winter!

SPONSOR A BLOOD DRIVE

Contact your local Red Cross and find out how to go about sponsoring a blood drive. They will help you from start to finish, from planning to the actual day of the drive. Invite the Media (newspapers and radio stations) to join you. Challenge schools or youth groups to see which group gets the most pints of blood donated. Contact a Pizza parlor beforehand and see if they will donate dinner for the winning group.

CELL PHONES TO LIFELINES

Donate your obsolete cell phones to a Homeless Shelter or a Shelter for Battered Women. They can still be used to make 911 Calls – giving a lifeline to someone who may desperately need it.

DAY 174 *Do not build a wall up today for something that happened yesterday. Do not push anyone away because you aren't brave enough to take a chance. Live like you are invincible and you will be.*

Just because you have the right doesn't mean it is right.

DAY 176 *Problems can always be solved no matter how big or small they are. Never hesitate to ask for help from anyone because someone out there will always be there to help you.*

_____
_____
_____
_____
_____
_____
_____
_____
_____
_____
_____
_____
_____
_____
_____
_____
_____
_____
_____
_____
_____
_____
_____
_____
_____
_____
_____
_____
_____

POWERFUL WOMAN STORY
High In the Sky

"Hey guess what I saw on Saturday?" Nicole squealed with delight. Her friends looked up from coloring their pictures and waited for her to answer.

"I went to an air show and saw a real fighter jet. It swooped through the sky and one day I am going to fly airplanes."

Nicole stopped talking then, stood and gazed out the school room window. Looking up to the sky, her imagination soared as the clouds wisped through the air. She could only imagine the feel of a real airplane beneath her hands. She dreamed and dreamed of soaring through the blue sky.

"Nicole? Nicole? Are you coming? We are going outside."

Her friends' call interrupted her dream but only temporarily. She knew what she wanted. All she had to do was look up to the sun and she knew where she would be...one day.

United States Air Force Major Nicole Malachowski was only 5 years old when she knew what she wanted to be when she grew up. She attended an air show and the sight of an F-4 Phantom fighter jet roaring through the clouds captured her heart and dreams. And once she set her sights on the sky, her feet have rarely been on the ground.

Nicole appreciates her parents' belief in her – in her dreams -- encouraging her tenacity and offering her courage to follow those dreams.

In an interview, Nicole remembers when she would ramble on about becoming a fighter pilot: *"They would often ask me rhetorical questions to get me thinking. Questions like, 'So you're going to be a fighter pilot? How does one become a fighter pilot?'"*

Nicole then figured out the answers . . . and instead of chasing boys through junior high, Nicole chased down pilot instructors, airplanes, flying lessons and cockpits. She starting flying at age 12 and flying solo by age 16! After school she rode her bike to the airport until she got her driver's license. She was flying before she could drive!!

Nicole is an amazing woman whose dreams have taken her literally to the top of the world.

After graduating from the Air Force Academy and working there as an instructor pilot, a conversation with her husband prompted her to land the wildest ride she had ever taken.

"Honey, you should try out. You're qualified. I think you might make it."

"Really? You really think I should apply? Really? Actually, I've not thought about that. But you really think I could?"

Her husband, Major Paul Malachowski, is no stranger to airplanes. As an F-15 weapons system officer evaluator, he was more than able to judge his wife's ability. With her husband's words of encouragement and his deep belief in her ringing in her ears, Nicole applied for, and was granted, a position with the elite and selective U.S. Air Force Air Demonstration Squadron . . . or as they are better known, the Thunderbirds.

With that selection, she flies into history books. Major Nicole Malachowski is the very first woman ever in its history, to pilot an F-16 Fighting Falcon.

"The Air Force has so many great opportunities out there, and all you have to do is apply," she said. *"It never hurts to try, does it?"*

WOW! This woman has inspired not only me, but thousands of people everywhere who watched her fly that screaming Falcon fighter jet across the noble blue skies. As a public relations organization for the Air Force, Nicole has spoken to hundreds of children across the globe. Her own words echo our mission here at I AM A POWERFUL WOMAN - pursue your dreams because they can come true!

"I hope (my) service in the Thunderbirds is an example to young girls and to all

children that they can achieve their dreams . . . it's great to have a dream; it's great to have goals," she said. *"Pursue something that you are passionate about, and then pursue excellence in that. And surround yourself with a positive team. I hope that when they see the Air Force Thunderbirds, they realize they can achieve any dream. I think I am living proof that dreams do come true."*

Today, you probably won't strap yourself into the cockpit of a Fighter jet and soar above the city. But you *can* step out into a world where your dreams of can come true.

You can begin today to take the steps needed to live out your heart's passion.

We are no different than Major Nicole Malachowski. She may skyrocket through the skies at top speeds, but her life is lived one day at a time. One goal at a time. One dream at a time. You can take on things the same way she does . . . one step at a time. If you don't quit and don't give up, then you, too, will reach the heights of our dreams!

DAY 177 *Dance like there's nobody watching; love like you'll never be hurt; sing like there's nobody listening; and live like it's heaven on earth.*

In three words I can sum up everything I've learned about life: it goes on.
~ Robert Frost

POWERFUL WOMAN ACTIONS

HORSE LOVERS NEEDED!

There are horse therapy organizations that need volunteers to help out with the horses. Sometimes volunteers walk alongside a therapy horse that is carrying a disabled child. Other times the horses need feeding, watering, currying, or their stables cleaned. There's always work to do where animals are present!

SNEAKY MOWER

Mow your neighbor's yard while they are at work. You can do it anonymously and leave them scratching their head (perhaps leaving an unsigned note asking them to "Pay it Forward", or you can leave a note telling them how glad you are that you're neighbors.

BE A COMPUTER ANGEL

If you have an old computer that still works take it to an elderly neighbor, then commit to teaching them how to operate it enough to send and receive email. Give them a connection to the world. What a great way for them to be connected to their family that is probably online. Their kids and grandkids will think they are so cool, and be so impressed that they mastered the computer! While you're at it become an E-mail Pen Pal with them yourself!

GRAFFITI CLEANER

Is there a lot of graffiti in your neighborhood or town? Get a group of friends

together and clean it up. Many times local Police Departments will supply the paint or special remover, depending on what you need. Be sure to get permission from the owners of the buildings or walls before doing any removal work.

DAY 180 *Insanity is doing the same thing, over and over again, but expecting different results.*

To LIVE is the rarest thing in the world. Most people exist, that is all.
    ~ Oscar Wilde

DAY 182 *It is better to be hated for what you are than to be loved for what you are not.*

She stood with her hands on the wall as her music teacher played notes on the kettledrum. Concentrating on the vibrations she was feeling, Evelyn knew what note she was playing by where she felt the vibration on her body. It felt good to be part of music again.

Evelyn remembers having perfect pitch and being able to sing a specific note without the aid of an instrument playing it for her. She loved playing the piano and clarinet. She smiles remembering when, at the age of 10, she performed on the piano in a local old folks home.

But with the loss of her hearing two years later, she now "heard" a note by associating where she feels it. Music is, as she points out, vibration, whether it's vibrating against your ear drum or another part of your body. *"The low sounds I feel mainly in my legs and feet, and high sounds might be particular places on my face, neck and chest."* She says that her feet, legs and tummy are her best ears.

Evelyn's passion for music was spurred on by one of her later music teachers who told her she could never pursue a career in music – after all, how could she, she couldn't even hear? Evelyn says that was one of the best things that ever happened to her because she became even more determined to make it happen. But Evelyn didn't want to be just a percussionist -- she wanted to be the featured artist – out in front and accompanied by the rest of the orchestra!

And she has done just that! After graduating from the Royal Academy of Music with honors, her career took flight. Helped by the press's love of the sentimental and emotional story of the plucky deaf teenager, Evelyn became a musical phenomenon. She produced six albums, performed concert tours in Asia, Europe and the U.S., and even became a TV talk show celebrity.

Evelyn may very possibly be the best percussionist in the world – she's definitely the first who has ever made a successful full-time career as a solo percussionist. She can play any kind of music – from classical to rock – and she is extremely innovative. When you watch and listen to Evelyn play, you have to leave all your preconceived ideas about deafness at the door. She doesn't *play* music – Evelyn *feels* and *becomes* the music. And her expressiveness pulls you right into the experience as well. About her music she says, *"That's me – that's my voice."*

Evelyn's won more than 80 international awards including a Grammy. She has been voted Scotswoman of the Decade and been awarded the Officer of the British Empire by Queen Elizabeth. That award has been extended to "Dame Commander" for her services to music. She can now be correctly called Dame Evelyn Glennie.

Evelyn's career has spanned more than 20 years and she has composed original works (as well as having original works composed specifically for her!). She has a grueling international touring schedule and often plays as many as 60 instruments during a single live performance.

Watching her makes you glad she didn't let her doctor or her music teacher steal her dream.

Have you ever experienced someone telling you something you felt strongly about couldn't be done? Have you ever shared a fantastic idea or goal with a family member or best friend and their immediate reaction was -- "that's

crazy"? With just two words spoken, your excitement comes crashing down around you and your idea, dream or goal lays at your feet, dashed into a thousand pieces.

Have you let others de-rail or limit you? Instead of following your dream, working on your idea or mapping out how to reach your goal, have you let someone else's opinion rob you of what's rightfully yours?

There are multitudes of people who were told they "couldn't do that" or "wouldn't succeed" but have ignored such comments and gone on to become wildly successful.

Some years ago Evelyn said: *"I have been a soloist for over ten years because I decided early on that just because my doctor made a diagnosis that I was profoundly deaf, it didn't mean that my passion couldn't be actualized. I would encourage people to not allow themselves to be defined or limited by others. Follow your passion; follow your heart. They will lead you to the place you want to go."* The next time someone tells you "that's crazy" just smile and ignore them.

Follow your dream -- no one can steal it unless you let them!

DAY 184 *It's a mistake to hold in higher esteem those who think alike than those who think differently.*

DAY 185 *Most people are not really free. They are confined by the niche in the world that they carve out for themselves. They limit themselves to few possibilities by the narrowness of their vision.*

DAY 186 *People willing to dilute themselves for the sake of others is one of the greatest tragedies of our time. Don't be peer pressured into being less than you are. Stop letting others define and set the pace for your life. Get out there and be your BEST. ~ Steve Maraboli*

POWERFUL WOMAN ACTIONS

ELDER ANGEL

Help someone who is elderly or sick by helping them around their home. You could paint; garden; mow lawn; shovel snow; take out trash. Just look around. You'll be able to discover what needs to be done.

Want to make *more* of an impact? Gather some of your friends and have an Elder Angel weekend. You'll be able to help so many more if you work together. If you need assistance finding people just talk to your local place of worship or volunteer center. There are so many in need!

SPREAD BEAUTY

Buy daffodil and tulip bulbs in the fall when they are cheapest and plant them at your school, church, neighbor's house, or anywhere else where their beauty can spread good feelings. You'll get the added benefit of enjoying them year after year.

YARD SALE FOR CHARITY

Have a garage sale and donate the proceeds to your favorite charity. You'll have to pay for signs and maybe some advertising, but it shouldn't be much.

You can also make this a joint effort. Talk to several families, or enlist your entire neighborhood by handing out flyers. You could also sweeten the pot a little by telling your neighbors to put up signs saying 50% of the proceeds will go to the charity you've decided to help. That way, they get to make some money, and also make a difference!

MAKE YOUR VOICE HEARD

Send Letters to the Editor at your local newspaper. Write about things in your community that you feel strongly about. Whenever writing such a letter, try to put your thoughts in a positive spin. Offer possible solutions to the problem, be specific. Help people see what you are seeing. Don't be offensive or complaining. State the facts, state your opinion, and then offer solutions. Make people think – but don't "make enemies" – keep communication open.

DAY 187 *It doesn't matter if I'm off the beat. It doesn't matter if I'm snapping to the rhythm. It doesn't matter if I look like a complete goon when I dance. It is my dance. It is my moment. It is mine. And dance I will. Try and stop me. You'll probably get kicked in the face. ~ Dan Pearce*

_____

_____

_____

_____

_____

_____

_____

_____

_____

_____

_____

_____

_____

_____

_____

_____

_____

_____

_____

_____

_____

_____

_____

_____

_____

_____

_____

_____

_____

DAY 189 *I will no longer let the fear of vicious comments or replies stop me from speaking what I believe to be right. I am done letting the bullies win. They won't anymore. Not here. ~ Amanda G.*

DAY 190 *Sometimes you don't realize your own strength until you come face to face with your greatest weakness.*

"Let's go guys...Ok...out the door...Time for your walk!"

"Easy...good girl...good boys!"

Victoria's enthusiasm always created excitement when she took the dogs out walking. As a professional dog walker in London, she had lots of onlookers. She usually literally had her hands full!

"Heel! Sit. Wait...wait...okay...go!" "Good dogs! Good dogs!" "Yeah!"

The sun shone brightly over the fragrant flower wall. The brightly colored blooms seem to turn their heads toward Victoria as she and her canine companions passed. She breathed in deeply . . . pondering whether or not she had discovered her niche in life. While the morning found her with three of her favorite dogs . . . three very well trained, obedient and joyous dogs, one of this

afternoon's appointments was an entirely different story. A story that occasionally gave Victoria doubts about her passion.

3:00 p.m. and it was time to go get her . . . the large, very ill-mannered dog she'd almost come to dread. Still she had hope her training techniques would work. She didn't get to see this dog everyday so progress was hard to gauge.

"Ok...sit! SIT! Good girl! Let's get your leash on! SIT! DOWN! Good girl! Ok...out!"

Hum," thought Victoria, *that was easier than usual. Let's see how the walk past the neighbor's dogs goes. WOW! She ignored them both! The training is working -- it IS working!*

"Perfect! Good girl!" her praise of her dog interrupted her thoughts.

The year was 1990 and Victoria Stilwell was then well on her way to becoming all she'd ever dreamed. A native of Wimbledon, England, Victoria now is one of the most recognized and respected dog trainers in the world.

Victoria started out her career walking dogs. When she saw her clients' need for help with their dog training problems, she sought further education and certification.

Simply, she saw a need in her business and decided she could be the one to fill it. She pursued something that would help her business but at the same time help her customers.

Victoria already had a passion for animals, dogs in particular, and combined her sensitive personality and her care for the humans with the open opportunity she saw existed. Even her background in theatre and stage was a plus as her popularity exceeded the local venues and she found herself before the bright lights of television.

Today, Victoria's TV show, "It's Me or the Dog" is viewed in over 20 countries worldwide. She literally goes into family's homes where there is great conflict between the two legged and the four legged companions. With grace, and smarts, she is filmed interacting and redirecting behavior of both the human and the dog. Victoria comes up against some of the most obnoxious animals I've ever encountered and yet she teaches everyone involved how to bring out the positive side of the animal. Sometimes she amazes even herself at how obedient these dogs can truly become.

Victoria is also an accomplished author, and a very sought after animal educator and trainer in her native England as well as New York and New Jersey, USA. She has been featured in magazines and TV shows around the world. Her expertise is craved internationally. Her advice, when heeded, can change people's lives. **Her** life has certainly evolved from walking dogs in her neighborhood.

Victoria is a perfect example of someone who creatively found success doing what she loves! It was not an overnight phenomenon . . . but she believed in her interests and desires. **She believed in herself and would not give up.** I know it wasn't easy and I am sure it still isn't easy for her today, to always "retrain" both the humans and their dogs to respect each other.

I'd be willing to bet for every successful show we watch, there are several that didn't turn out quite as well. But you know, Victoria takes a few steps forward in giving, and learning and pursuing every time she ventures out into a new family's life.

You could do that too. Oh, maybe not retrain dogs in 2 countries, but you can take a few steps toward your goals. *And you can decide to not give up!* You can look at what you really love to do and find ways to make that a bigger part of your life. You can choose to believe in yourself!!

DAY 191 *Beliefs have the power to create and the power to destroy. Human beings have the awesome ability to take any experience of their lives and create a meaning that disempowers them or one that can literally save their lives.* ~ Tony Robbins

DAY 192 *Courage doesn't always roar. Sometimes courage is the quiet voice at the end of the day say, "I will try again tomorrow." ~ Mary Ann Radmacher*

DAY 193   *The brave may not live forever, but the cautious don't live at all.*
~ Ashley L.

BE A COACH!

Coach an after-school or summer sports team for kids. Check with the YMCA, local volunteer center, or city recreation department for ways to "plug in." Gather a few friends and make it a true team effort. You'll be making a huge impact on the kids while you have fun at the same time. Encourage parents to provide refreshments after the games. And make sure EVERY kid gets to play regardless of his or her skill level.

HOMELESS KIDS

Did you know that national statistics report the number of homeless kids at over 1.5 million? And over 500 thousand are under the age of 15 – some even as young as 9 years old! Why not pack up some sack lunches and go walk the

city streets with some friends – or other youth? Give lunches to the homeless kids you meet. Take time to talk with them. Maybe you can help steer them toward the help they need. But mostly, just let them know someone cares.

Go to StandUp For Kids (www.standupforkids.org) and see if there is a group already doing this where you can get training and support. Or contact your city police department. Many have neighborhood offices where you can volunteer and reach the kids that way.

STAND UP FOR KIDS

Have a drive to collect items for homeless and street kids. Stand Up For Kids always needs clothing, hygiene products, food and other resources to hand out to the kids on the streets. Visit their website for more information.

ANIMAL FOSTER HOME

You can help free an animal from a Shelter – providing foster care until they can be adopted out to the right family. You will receive unlimited love and the powerful knowledge you have helped save the life of a helpless animal! Just call your local shelter – either your city Humane Shelter, or a local no-kill shelter. Most areas have more than one.

DAY 194 *Anyone can give up; it's the easiest thing in the world to do. But to hold it together when everyone else would understand if you fell apart, that's true strength.*

_____

_____

_____

_____

_____

_____

_____

_____

_____

_____

_____

_____

_____

_____

_____

_____

_____

_____

_____

_____

_____

_____

_____

_____

_____

DAY 194 *Anyone can give up; it's the easiest thing in the world to do. But to hold it together when everyone else would understand if you fell apart, that's true strength.*

POWERFUL WOMAN STORY
From Welfare to Billionaire

Glancing at the baby sweetly sleeping in her stroller Jo thought to herself, *"I hope she sleeps awhile longer."* Strange -- the dips and turns life takes. She never thought she'd find herself on welfare, but here she was. Walking her daughter in the stroller so she'd fall asleep, Jo would then take refuge in a café to write.

When she closed her eyes, she saw her story's characters come to life. The trick now was capturing them and putting them on paper! She smiled, letting her mind drift and remembering the first story she'd ever written down . . . she was about 6 years old and the story was about a rabbit that caught the measles and was visited by his friends, including a giant bee.

Born in England, Jo basically grew up on the border of Wales. Although not a good student, she loved reading and writing. After graduating from college, she moved to London and worked for Amnesty International doing research on human rights abuse in Africa.

The baby stirred and Jo held her breath – ah, good, she went back to sleep...

Jo remembered the crowded train trip where the idea for her book came to her in its complete form. *"I really don't know where the idea came from... all these characters and situations came flooding into my head."* As soon as she got to her apartment, she started writing. The year was 1990.

In December of the same year, Jo's 40 year-old mother died after a ten-year battle with multiple sclerosis. She never knew Jo had started work on a novel. Deeply affected by her mother's death, nine months later Jo moved to Portugal where she taught English in a language institute. While there she married a Portuguese television journalist and their daughter, Jessica, was born in 1993. When they divorced the next year, Jo and Jessica moved to Edinburgh, Scotland to be near her sister.

This was a very difficult time for Jo. Choosing not to return to teaching full-time, she went on welfare so she could continue writing. She knew *"that unless I finished the book very soon, I might never finish it . . . and so I set to work in a kind of frenzy, determined to finish the book and at least try and get it published."* Unable to afford an electric typewriter (much less a computer), Jo first wrote in long hand and then typed the story on a manual typewriter.

Sitting in that café, watching her daughter sleep and writing her books, Jo had no idea what was to come . . .

Once the first book, the *Philosopher's Stone,* was completed and she found an agent, it took another year of rejection after rejection before finding a publisher. Finally, in August of 1996, her agent called to tell her he'd found a company to publish her book. *"After I hung up, I screamed and jumped into the air; Jessica, who was sitting in her high-chair . . . looked thoroughly scared."*

The world would soon become entranced with Harry Potter and his adventures. (It's interesting to note that against Jo's wishes, the U.S. publisher insisted on renaming the book the *Sorcerer's Stone*.)

J. K. Rowling (pronounced roll-ing) has been named by *Forbes* as the first person to become a U.S.-dollar billionaire by writing books, that she's the second-richest female entertainer and the 1,062nd richest person in the world. Jo had no idea her Harry Potter books would become the worldwide phenomenon that they are. She is uncomfortable in the limelight and is much happier giving to others than she is speaking about herself. Jo is very involved in helping women and children around the world - combating poverty and supporting multiple sclerosis research.

J.K. Rowling is a success because she never gave up. For 6 long years she lived with very little in order to push her dream forward. It was when things were the worst that she clung to the belief that the stories she was writing were meant to be read. And millions of readers around the world have proven her right.

You and I may never be famous. We may never be known beyond our family and friends. But each of us is important. And each of us has a dream. We can choose to be true to our dream, and like Jo Rowling, do whatever it takes to achieve it.

DAY 198 *Strength does not come from winning. Your struggles develop your strengths. When you go through hardships and decide not to surrender, that is strength.*

_____

_____

_____

_____

_____

_____

_____

_____

_____

_____

_____

_____

_____

_____

_____

_____

_____

_____

_____

_____

_____

_____

_____

_____

_____

_____

_____

_____

_____

DAY 199 *Anyone can hide. Facing up to things, working through them, that's what makes you strong. ~ Sarah Dessen*

AUDUBON SOCIETY

Join your local Audubon Society. They always need volunteers to:

- help with educational programs in elementary schools
- guide and assist in nature walks
- lead outdoor, nature-themed after-school programs
- help plan and implement events and activities at local preserves
- take part in documenting activities and events (taking pictures and writing for their newsletters)

PET SITTING

Provide a free Pet Sitting Service. Often when people go on vacation or long business trips they need someone to watch their pets. Why not get a group of friends together to start the service so you can feed pets, take them for walks, and play with them. Animals love their people and miss them when they're gone. Your Pet Babysitting Service could save them from having to spend that time in a cage at a boarding facility.

SPECIAL OLYMPICS

Volunteer to help your local Special Olympics. Did you know that the Special Olympics Athlete Oath is: *Let me win. But if I cannot win, let me be brave in the attempt.* That's a great oath for life in general, don't you think? You can volunteer for just one event or you give several hours a week/month throughout the year. There are several levels of involvement including the state/provincial, national or international level. You might help present awards, be a scorekeeper or assist with food service. There is always plenty to do. To determine where to start, visit the Special Olympics website at www.SpecialOlympics.org and click on the Volunteer tab.

DAY 201 *Courage is looking fear right in the eye and saying, "Get out of my way, I've got things to do."*

_____

_____

_____

_____

_____

_____

_____

_____

_____

_____

_____

_____

_____

_____

_____

_____

_____

_____

_____

_____

_____

_____

_____

_____

_____

_____

DAY 202 *If you always put limits on everything you do, physical or anything else, it will spread throughout your life. There are no limits. There are only plateaus; you must not stay there, you must go beyond them.*

DAY 205 *Courage is what it takes to stand up and speak; courage is also what it takes to sit down and listen.* ~ *Winston Churchill*

"I hate this dress! And I hate this fashion!" Ida yelled passionately to her husband as she dressed.

A buxom woman living in the 1920's, Ida had a hard time adjusting to the "flat chested" look of the day. She was a visionary and a self-made woman. Ida knew what she wanted and she began to go after it. She emigrated from Russia to marry her boyfriend who had immigrated a few years earlier. They started with no money . . . they had nothing but a dream of a better life in the USA and they had Ida's irritation with American fashion.

"Ida . . . are you through yet?" asked her William. *"The ad agency is waiting.*

"Yes, I am nearly through with this round. Tell them I will bring it all by their office on Monday."

Not fitting into the current fashion known as "Boyish form," Ida asked the question: *"Why fight nature?" Why couldn't we make something that actually FITS a woman's body?"*

Not only did she ask the question – she had the means to provide the answer. An avid Women's Rights Activist, she had long ago turned up her nose to the idea of working for someone else. Instead, she bought a Singer sewing machine on the installment plan and began her own seamstress business.

In 1921, when women were "wrapping their breasts," Ida started her own dress shop in Manhattan. She thought women could look better in their dresses and set about to do something about it. She and her husband, William, designed built-in bandeaux with cups that separated and supported the breasts. They were an instant hit.

The women's bra company Maiden Form was born.

Ida was the management and marketing genius behind their success. She bought ads, negotiated with Unions and introduced assembly-line production. She pushed the boundaries by running "racy" ads featuring photographs of women in bras.

Ida Rosenthal proved female executives could succeed at a time when working women rarely got further than factory worker or secretary. The bras she helped create liberated women with comfort, freedom and sensuality. They also created multimillionaires of Ida and William.

Ida is a shining light of what can be accomplished if you keep your eyes open, recognize a need, and set out to do something about it!

I don't care how long you live. I don't care how advanced society becomes. I don't care how many inventions are invented. There are always problems to solve; solutions to be presented; easier ways to do things. You just have to believe it. You just have to keep your eyes open for the opportunity that ignites your passion and purpose.

Next time you feel that wave of frustration about *"how things are done"* . . . look at the situation again. Do you see a better way? An easier way to accomplish that task? A more productive solution?

If so, then pursue getting things changed. Ida believed she had a better idea . . . a more comfortable way for women to live. And she simply lived out her dreams and passions.

Living out dreams and passions – what a sure-fire way to live as a Powerful Woman!

Above all, be the heroine of your life, not the victim.

_____
_____
_____
_____
_____
_____
_____
_____
_____
_____
_____
_____
_____
_____
_____
_____
_____
_____
_____
_____
_____
_____
_____
_____
_____
_____
_____
_____
_____
_____

DAY 208 *Courage is when you know you're licked before you begin, but you begin anyway and see it through no matter what.* ~ *Atticus Finch*

YOUTH AROUND THE WORLD

You can inspire youth to make a difference! Learn how youth are making their voices heard around the world on the Voices of Youth website. This site is sponsored by UNICEF and enables youth to make their voices heard at the UN level. They offer forums for your opinions and sometimes host round-table discussions with youth and UN leaders. They do listen to what you say – and they publish the impact your participation is making on behalf of children and youth around the world. Visit www.Unicef.org/voy and get involved.

TAKE A BITE OUT OF CRIME!

Want to "take a bite out of crime"? Visit the National Crime Prevention Council's website (www.ncpc.org). Click on the Resources tab and become part of more than a million people creating safer schools and neighborhoods. Understand how crime affects you and your family, friends and community and get involved in crime prevention projects. You can download their gang fact sheets right from the site.

PRESERVE HISTORY

Is there a historic building in your town that needs some repair work? Help preserve a piece of your area's history by organizing a group of people (be sure to include the Historical Society in your town) to get it fixed up. You'll need to get appropriate permission, but you'll find the Historical Society will help in every way they can to support your project! Invite the newspapers and radio stations to get involved, too! You can be proud of this for the rest of your life!

DAY 209   *Courage is not the absence of fear, but rather the judgment that something else is more important than fear.*

DAY 212   *Have enough courage to trust love one more time, and always one more time.*

_____

_____

_____

_____

_____

_____

_____

_____

_____

_____

_____

_____

_____

_____

_____

_____

_____

_____

_____

_____

_____

_____

_____

_____

_____

_____

_____

_____

_____

Do you follow the Olympics?

Interested in trivia about sporting events?

Can you answer these questions then?

Who broke World Record in the women's 50 m freestyle swimming event THREE times in the early 1980's?

Who won five medals alone in the Sydney Olympics in 2000?

Who is the first swimmer to compete in five Olympics: 1984, 1988, 1992, 2000, and 2008?

Who was the oldest female swimmer ever in its history, at 41 years of age to compete in the Bejing Summer Olympics – taking home 3 Silver medals?

Who won the heart of America when she missed the Gold in Bejing by 1/100th of a second – mesmerizing us with her astonishing achievement **and** *her good-natured acceptance of the results?*

Who has inspired many older athletes to re-enter competition because they've seen what is possible?

The answer to all these questions is Dara Torres, swimmer phenomenon.

Dara started swimming in Beverly Hills, California because her brothers swam at the local YMCA. But that sibling rivalry turned competitive as Dara learned to win. At age 14, she broke the world record in the 50-meter freestyle, but wasn't too impressed with herself or her record. What impressed her was that she didn't lose. Coming in 2nd or 3rd is nearly unbearable to this tanned, tall woman with an easy laugh.

Her family and friends know she doesn't necessarily play to win but she plays hard so as to not lose. Her biggest competition is not the competitor on the next starting block but the woman within. She likes to improve her time, her form and her body!

Even though she has retired from competitive swimming, Dara hasn't slowed down. She is devoted to her daughter, works as a broadcaster, television network announcer & model, and also maintains peak physical fitness.

Dara pursued her first love of swimming through single determination and purpose. She never allowed herself to quit. It is not without pain or obstacles... Injuries, bone spurs, torn muscles, and even 10+ surgeries didn't deter her path.

Her family and friends have nailed her personality *"'. . . Dara's personality is not type A. She's type A + +."*

Dara Torres won so many hearts because she refused to accept the limitations others set for her.   In Bejing she competed with swimmers around 20 years younger than she was – and brought home 3 medals!

She refused to let anyone else determine her possibilities – she made her dreams come true.

You may not be able to keep up with her, or her grueling schedule, or physical feats, but you can mimic her focus on pursing her passion. You can keep trying, keep going, and keep moving toward the goal!

You can do it!

You may not be on the starters' block of an Olympic event, but you *are* in the event of life and you have many life races to join.

You might lose some but ultimately you'll win if you keep on keeping on!!

DAY 213 *It's never too late, or too early, to be whoever you want to be. You can change or stay the same – there are no rules to this thing called life. If you find you're living a life you're not proud of, I hope you have the courage to start all over again. ~ Eric Roth*

DAY 215 *At times the world may seem an unfriendly and sinister place, but believer there is much more good in it than bad. All you have to do is look hard enough, and what might seem to be a series of unfortunate events may in fact be the first steps of a journey.*

_____
_____
_____
_____
_____
_____
_____
_____
_____
_____
_____
_____
_____
_____
_____
_____
_____
_____
_____
_____
_____
_____
_____
_____
_____
_____
_____
_____

FREE PASSES

Approach your local performing arts center to give Free passes to events – then give them to children at a Safe House or Shelter. Giving them a chance to see what is in the world besides the reality of their own situation will make a huge difference.

ARE YOU AN ARTIST?

There are hundreds of underprivileged kids who don't have access to art

 classes or materials. Get some of your art classes to offer after school art classes at one of the poorer schools, YMCAs or community centers in your community. Provide the materials and teach the kids what you know. At the end of the classes provide an art show featuring your students' work. Open it to the neighborhood and invite the media to attend. Make the world a better place through art – open the world of art to kids who wouldn't know it without you.

SPONSOR A HOLOCAUST REMEMBRANCE DAY IN APRIL

One of the most horrific events in our modern history was the Holocaust in Germany from 1933 to 1945, some 60 years ago. Fewer and fewer of the survivors remain alive to talk about their experiences, but we need to remember that over 6 million people were exterminated in the name of creating a superior race. Visit the United States Holocaust Memorial Museum online at www.ushmm.org for more information.

HELP WITH HEALTH CARE FAIRS

Contact your local Community Outreach Center and volunteer to help with their Health Care Fair (or whatever they call it at their Center). There will be all kinds of things to do: pass out flyers, help people with directions, help direct traffic in the parking lot, make posters, help set up, help clean up afterwards, etc.

**my life
my health**

DAY 216   *My great hope is to laugh as much as I cry; to get my work done and try to love somebody and have the courage to accept the love in return.*
   ~ Maya Angelou

DAY 217 *Don't be afraid of your fears. They're not there to scare you. They're there to let you know that something is worth it. ~ C. JoyBell*

DAY 218   *There is a stubbornness about me that never can bear to be frightened at the will of others. My courage always rises at every attempt to intimidate me.*
~ Jane Austen

DAY 219   *Courage isn't the strength to go on – it's going on when you don't have the strength. ~ Napoleon Bonaparte*

The surf crashed onto the sandy beach and the sun seemed to halt in the middle of the sky. White wispy clouds framed the water and everyone was having fun. Relaxing with a boogie board, the beach was a favorite place for Chanda. Water has a calming effect and this California girl was no stranger to the waves. Yet the dilemma of Chanda's health tainted the day. Watching their children romping and rolling on the beach, her parents, though silent on the outside thought the same thoughts...

What if she is in the water and she has a seizure?

What if no one sees her?

She could die!

She's only 9... why does she have to have epilepsy? I wonder if we should go home?

What if she can't tell us she needs help?

The splashing the kids created was matched by their boisterous laughter and soon the parental worries ceased. However, they both knew they would have to talk about it soon. Chanda was still so young and many decisions would need to be made but for now, their greatest choice was which kid to toss into the wild waves rushing into shore.

Chanda Gunn and her parents ultimately decided it was in her best interest and safety to not pursue water sports. At that young age, she had multiple seizures daily. The water in its liquid form was simply too dangerous for her. As they dropped off her brother at hockey, they wondered if water in its frozen form could be their answer to Chanda's desire to play sports. It seemed with the protective helmet and gear, that she would be safe if a seizure did hit her.

It proved to be a perfect match. In fact, she is the first player to be a finalist for the nation's best women's college hockey player (The Patty Kazmaier Award) and an award as college hockey's finest citizen (The Humanitarian). She's also received the Honda Inspiration Award. In 2005 she was voted top goalie in the world championships. Her team won the gold! In 2006 at the Winter Olympics, she won a bronze medal. There she played around 250 minutes. She had 50 saves. This two-time All-America goaltender is as at home on the ice as she was in the waves.

"Chanda was an extremely shy, quiet child until she put on goalie pads. Then her entire personality changed. She grew tremendously confident and showed abilities I had no idea she had," Chanda's mother reflected on her daughter in a recent interview.

This tough gal has her epilepsy under control and uses her sports fame to speak to groups, especially kids whenever she gets the chance.

Her advice to parents or kids themselves with any kind of challenge is steeped with experience.

"'Of course, children with epilepsy may have a more difficult time, but if they are told they 'can't' or they 'shouldn't' they are going to grow up always feeling unsure, and may not try new things. By letting your child participate in a sport you are letting them be accountable for themselves and also enabling them to view the handicap they have as less of a handicap, and more as something they deal with.'"

Her attitude is great and from what I can tell, she certainly walks the walk of someone who should know. I think it is inspiring to know that Chanda lives her life with the conviction that she can do anything she wants. She may have to try harder or handle some things differently, but she is able. She is definitely capable!

I want you to know that too. You don't have to pull on a goalie helmet to take on discouragement or disappointment. Chanda could have sulked when her parents took her out of swimming and set her down on frozen ground. But she didn't. She simply chose to be the best she could be and look at her go!!

Today, be like Chanda and choose to be your best!!

One's dignity may be assaulted, vandalized and cruelly mocked, but it can never be taken away unless it is surrendered

DAY 222 *If you are neutral in situations of injustice, you have chosen the side of the oppressor. If an elephant has its foot on the tail of a mouse, and you say that you are neutral, the mouse will not appreciate your neutrality.*
     ~ Desmond Tutu

BE A VIRTUAL VOLUNTEER

If it's difficult for you to leave your home, but you have access to a computer, research the possibilities for being a virtual volunteer. It's very important that you be careful and make sure the company is legitimate. Be very wary if they ask you for money – it's a good chance they are scamming you. Since it's virtual volunteering, your communication will mostly be through email, although you may use the telephone for communicating with your supervisor and phone conferences.

You might write articles, create layouts for websites, and maybe even help in recruiting other volunteers. And many times you can come up with your own ideas of what you'd like to do to help the organization. And the best part is you can do your volunteering any time – even in your pajamas and no one will know! Visit www.dosomething.org/volunteer/virtual for some ideas.

GREEN THUMB SERVICE

Do you have a "green thumb"? Adopt a local emergency shelter or low-income nonprofit organization that can't afford to hire gardeners and take care of their current yard or vegetation. Even if they are a street-front location, there are usually some plants to care for. If not, gather some friends together and beautify their location with plants in containers. Then be sure to keep going back every week (or as needed) to water and care for the vegetation.

ANIMAL LOVER

If you have a "way with animals," volunteer at your veterinarian's clinic. There

are always cages to clean, bandages to change, and animals that are missing "their people" who would benefit from a friendly voice and some petting. There will most likely be other activities they'll need your help with, like rabies clinics, community pet adoptions, etc.

323

DAY 223   *Some people won't be happy until they've pushed you to the ground. What you have to do is have the courage to stand your ground and not give them the time of day. Hold on to your power and never give it away.*
~ *Donna Schoenrock*

I would rather be a little nobody, than be an evil somebody.

DAY 225 *What if the kid you bullied at school, grew up, and turned out to be the only surgeon who could save your life? ~ Lynette Mather*

When people see you're happy doing what you're doing, it sort of takes the power away from them to tease you about it. ~ Wendy Mass

"I can't do this anymore. I am through."

'You have to get an education, Terra."

"No, I don't. I quit."

"You don't realize how important it is. Quitting so close to graduating high school will haunt you for the rest of your life. You only have 2 years left."

"I quit. I don't care. I can't learn it. I just want out."

Terra Williams walked out of her high school as a dropout and entered the real world full time. She moved and made a life far away from her home and family. She struggled to make a life for herself and then her first daughter. Then her second daughter. Now a third daughter. Without a high school education, finances were tough. The years passed and as Terra matured, she longed for better.

"Mom? I can't do this anymore out here. There are drugs everywhere. I'm afraid for the girls. They won't always be so young and innocent. I hate this life. I don't want them growing up with drugs on every corner."

"Come home then, Terra. If you are not satisfied with your life, then do something different, baby, so you can go make a better life. I will support you however you need. I know you can make a better life for all of you. Just come home."

Terra moved back home to South Dakota, USA and to her home within the Sioux Nation.

Trouble was, Terra still didn't have that high school education. Therefore, she bravely enrolled herself and her girls in the *FACE* program. *FACE* stands for Family and Child Education. Funded through the Bureau of Indian Education, it is a family literacy program for Native Americans.

"I was so happy and really scared at first to be in our new home and going to a new school where we knew no one. I remember the first day of school for Destinee and me. We sat in the parking lot and I thought 'Are we ready for this?'"

Terra and her girls were ready. They have all excelled. The oldest girl is now in the Gifted and Talented program in math and science at her school. The middle child proudly displays her reading chart indicating the minutes she reads *every day!!* She loves to learn new words. The youngest child showed some learning problems as a toddler but she is rapidly catching up. And Terra?

While she is still studying for her G.E.D. (General Educational Development) she recently found herself on an airplane (for the very first time) flying to Colorado for a national convention as a speaker! As a national FACE parent essay winner, she addressed hundreds of people at FACE National Training. Amazing! Can you believe it!

She is a public speaker, when only a few months earlier she was struggling to learn.

"...and it was very emotional for me. I thought that was scary, but never in my life did I imagine speaking before this huge crowd at another national conference."

I love stories like this! Terra's future is bright. Her girls' lives are full of hope.

Terra could have closed her mind and her heart to education and her home.

Now she is writing books in her native Dakotah language. She dreams of preserving that aspect of her Native American heritage. Her dreams are coming true.

Be like Terra and do whatever it takes to make your dreams come true!

Never do a wrong thing to make a friend – or to keep one.

_____
_____
_____
_____
_____
_____
_____
_____
_____
_____
_____
_____
_____
_____
_____
_____
_____
_____
_____
_____
_____
_____
_____
_____
_____
_____
_____
_____
_____
_____

DAY 228   *Often, the right path is the one that may be the hardest for you to follow. But the hard path is also the one that will make you grow as a human being. ~ Karen Mueller Coombs*

There is no gesture more devastating than the back turning away.

LIFE STORIES

Volunteer to tape record the life stories of hospice patients. Hospice is a program that comes alongside people who are dying. These individuals have a story to tell about their life. Gather some friends together, get tape recorders and interview them; letting them tell their stories. Create some art to go with each individual's story and give it to them to share with their families. Perhaps the hospice program would like a copy, too. The Hospice program you're working with will want to give you training before you start your project.

SET ANOTHER PLACE AT THE TABLE

Invite someone who is lonely to all your family celebrations. Make sure they know you aren't just reaching out to them because they are lonely – let them

know you really WANT them with you. Everyone longs to know they are important and wanted. It doesn't have to be anything fancy – just full of love and warm feelings!

MIGRANT WORKERS

If you live in an area where there are migrant workers, put together a program for the children of the workers. Enlist the community center and area churches to give you a place to meet, then play games, make crafts, etc. Without a program like this, many of these kids would be left in hot cars all day while their parents work.

DAY 230 *Whenever you're got a choice, do good. It isn't always fun or easy, but in the long run it makes your life better.*

DAY 231 *Words have great power that can make or break others – please use yours with great care.*

Sometimes good things fall apart so that better things can fall together.

"This is so disturbing!" Albina looked at the polluted river and vacant lots filled with trash and reeking of garbage.

"Hey, don't dump your garbage there!" The youngster shrugs as she throws the trash and runs.

Albina Ruiz became aware of the growing problem of the lack of effective waste management in her native Peru while studying industrial engineering. After receiving her masters in Ecological and Environmental Management, she came up with an idea. What if she could create a community-managed waste collection system?

Albina chose El Cono Norte in Lima as her neighborhood guinea pig. She knew the municipality's waste collection was able to process only half of the community's trash. Not only did people not use the service, when they did, they rarely paid their bills. It was a vicious cycle.

People were tossing their garbage in the streets, rivers and vacant lots. The result was not only a smelly, ugly environment – it was also causing serious health problems. People were not only getting sick from their groundwater being contaminated, they also were being negatively affected psychologically by the whole situation.

Her idea was fairly simple -- find entrepreneurs – small business people – who would take charge of collecting and processing the garbage. This would result in two things: more efficient waste management and reverse unemployment. Albina helped people (mostly women) set up their businesses. They arrived at the fee of $1.50 a month for the service. Next she came up with all kinds of creative marketing ideas – including gift baskets – to get families to use the service AND pay each month on time.

The new business owners go door-to-door collecting garbage and the fees, while educating people about the importance of respecting and protecting their environment. Some of these entrepreneurs have even built profitable secondary businesses by creating products like organic fertilizer out of the trash they collect.

Albina started this project (Ciudad Saludable – Healthy City) nearly 20 years ago and now oversees projects in 20 cities across Peru. She employs more than 150 people, has over 4,000 small business owners, and serves over 4 million residents. Her model is so successful she has been asked to create a national plan for Peru. Other Latin American countries have also expressed interest in her program.

Albina stays in contact with the people within her organization. She still visits other cities overwhelmed by garbage, checks in on the neighborhoods involved in her program and meets with government officials.

Albina says, *"Where most people see a problem – I see a possibility."* And her ultimate goal is to change the way people think.

Do you see a problem you can turn into a possibility? You don't have to tackle it alone – ask for help! There are a lot of people who will come alongside you – and there are a lot of possibilities out there needing creative people to solve them!!

Be like Albina and create solutions every chance you get. It's often in working on a solution, that you'll end up making new friends – and learn a lot in the process!

And isn't that what being a POWERFUL WOMAN is all about? Learning – relationships – and giving back!

DAY 234 *Too many women buy things they don't need with money they don't have to impress people they don't know.*

DAY 235 *No matter how many mistakes you make or how slow you progress, you are still way ahead of everyone who isn't trying.*

LISTEN TO WHAT ONE GROUP OF FRIENDS DID...

Last summer 50 of my friends and I went to the Community Center. We

painted it, fixed the chairs, and basketball hoops; we bought some more balls and equipment with the money we raised from School Rummage and Bake Sale. We repainted the lines on the courts and planted some flowering plants in front.

Another group of us repaired the Jungle-Gym, the slide and the swings out back. Then we painted all of them rainbow colors and weeded the back lot.

We had a lot of fun and I know we made a difference!

VISUALLY-IMPAIRED

Read to a visually-impaired person. Go to the library and bring them books on tape – returning them when they are ready for more. The elderly spend so much time alone. To be alone in a dark world with nothing to do is so very difficult. You can make a massive difference to these people.

BIRD HOUSES

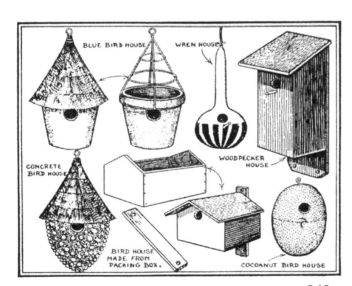

Build Bird Houses and put them everywhere you can. Inviting extra birds to your community is always a good thing. Just some of the benefits include:
- Pest Control
- Pollination
- Weed Control
- Food Sharing
- Increased Property Value
- Environmental Conservation

DAY 236 *Making one person smile can change the world – maybe not the whole world, but their world.*

Life is 10% of what happens to you, and 90% of how you react to it.

DAY 239   *As we grow up we realize it becomes less important to have more friends, and more important to have* real *ones.*

"But, Mom, I want to see the world and speak to millions. I want to travel and be a world changer."

"Cynthia, now, now, be realistic, dear. You're a girl from the Midwestern U.S. You need to play it safe and be practical. There's a job opening downtown for a secretary. Try that and don't be so dreamy. You need to know you can support yourself. Don't be so idealistic, sweetie. Just be realistic. You know I love you."

Cynthia got her first job as a secretary.

"Cynthia, I am sorry but we are going to have to let you go."

She got a second job as a secretary.

Cynthia, I'm sorry but we need to reorganize the business, so you will be moving down.

After finding a job with a little less demand for attention to "detail," Cynthia stayed for ten years as a National Account Manager for a large U.S. telephone service provider. She worked and went to school to get her degree. In addition, she grew weary of the corporate atmosphere.

Her desire grew to write a book. She desired to capture all the people she studied that did extraordinary things with horrific obstacles. Cynthia knew about hundreds of people who were "unstoppable." They never quit. They tried repeatedly. And eventually she saw where they were successful.

Had she ever *written* a book? No.

Did she know *how* to write a book? No.

Did she have a publisher? No.

However, the next phone call went something like this.

"You've done what? You quit your job and sold your house? Why? Cynthia, what are you thinking? Where are you going to live? You are going to do what?

Your savings? You took out your savings? Oh my, Cynthia have you gone mad?"

Cynthia did just that and leased a home 1/2 the size of her original and began writing.

Why make such drastic changes? So that I could be unstoppable in creating something that was really meaningful for me."

Meet Cynthia Kersey, *best-selling author, coach, speaker, consultant and expert in the field of human potential* **AND** CEO of Unstoppable Enterprises.

Cynthia has an entire business of helping others reach their dreams. She understands risk, failure, mistakes, and challenges. She has faced them all. When you hear her speak, she speaks of trying over and then over again. Taking things slowly...one step at a time.

"I've interviewed enough unstoppable

people over the last 10 years to say unequivocally that unstoppable people get frustrated, disappointed, discouraged, and even have moments of depression, and yet they don't quit. So, it's not that they're so different. They just don't make it mean that, when they have difficulties, it's 'game over.' They don't make it mean, 'I'm not good enough.' They might think it just for a moment, but they'll dispute it, and they'll continue to move forward."

You can be like Cynthia. "Unstoppable." You may not have all the answers or know exactly what your next step will look like. That is ok. Just as long as you keep making another step! Never quit! Never, ever!

*** There is something else very special about Cynthia Kersey. It wasn't enough for her to help change individual lives; she also has a passion to change the world through EDUCATION – giving the opportunity to learn to children all around the world.

Her passion led her to start **The Unstoppable Foundation**, which has been responsible for dozens of schools being built, and thousands of children having a chance to learn.

The Unstoppable Foundation is one of the organizations that received funding when you (or someone who cares about you) bought you this journal! Every time someone buys a POWERFUL WOMAN JOURNAL, a child somewhere in the world gets the chance for an education.

Now that's what I call POWERFUL!

_____

_____

_____

_____

_____

_____

_____

_____

_____

_____

_____

_____

_____

_____

_____

_____

_____

_____

_____

_____

_____

_____

_____

_____

_____

_____

DAY 241 *Giving up doesn't always mean you're weak; sometimes it means you are strong enough and smart enough to let go and move on.*

DAY 242 *If you really want to do something, you'll find a way. If you don't, you'll find an excuse.*

MUSIC ANYONE??

Do you play a musical instrument? Offer to teach someone. Maybe it's a kid who can't afford lessons on their own. Maybe it's someone who is housebound. Maybe it's an elderly person who has always dreamed of playing the piano – or some other instrument.

VOLUNTEER MATCH

RUN to your computer and check out http://www.VolunteerMatch.org. But beware... once you have been here you will never have an excuse for not volunteering. ☺ Volunteer Match is a nonprofit organization with a mission to help everyone find a great place to volunteer, and offers a variety of online services to support a community of nonprofit, volunteer and business leaders committed to civic engagement. Interested volunteers can enter their ZIP code on the Volunteer Match home page to quickly find local volunteer opportunities posted by nonprofit organizations throughout the United States.

NEW KIDS

Gather some friends/neighbors together and discuss your community. Make a list of the best things in your town – where to shop, restaurants, theaters, parks, nearby attractions. Include things to do that don't cost anything, too. Have someone take notes and compile the list. Then when someone new moves into your neighborhood, or starts at your school, take it to them with a "welcome" plate of cookies or some other goodies. You'll be surprised how many new friends you make and it sure makes being the new person a whole lot easier!

DAY 244   *True love isn't about being inseparable; it's about two people being true to each other even when they're separate.*

Discover the Best-Selling Bregdan Chronicles...

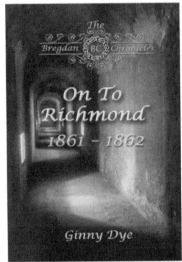

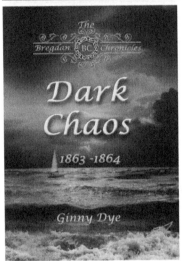

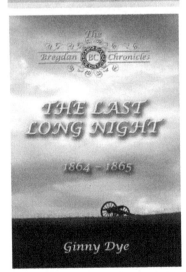

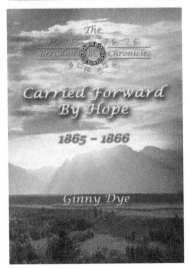

Historical fiction at its best!

www.BregdanChronicles.com

DAY 245 *While you're busy looking for the perfect person, you'll probably miss the imperfect person who could make you perfectly happy.*

_____

_____

_____

_____

_____

_____

_____

_____

_____

_____

_____

_____

_____

_____

_____

_____

_____

_____

_____

_____

_____

_____

_____

_____

_____

_____

Let me share my favorite story about perseverance. Have you ever heard of Maxcy Filer? Probably not -- I hadn't.

Maxcy Filer was married with two young sons when he decided to become an attorney. He'd been inspired by two attorneys who were making positive changes in the laws of his community and he wanted to be part of that change. Maxcy was 36 years old.

So he went to law school, graduated, and took the bar exam. Like many others before him he failed on the first try. So Maxcy took it again. Well, he continued to take it throughout his sons' undergraduate schooling. And he continued to take it while they attended and graduated from law school. And yes, he continued to take it after he was working for his sons as a law clerk in their offices!

Finally, after 25 years and 47 attempts, Maxcy Filer passed the bar exam at the age of 61. While most people were retiring, he began living his dream.

What do *you* do when you get discouraged? I hope the next time you face discouragement, you'll remember Maxcy Filer.

"Keep on keepin' on" and you'll come out on the other side – living as a Powerful Woman!

The difference between a quitter and someone persistent, is one tiny moment.

The quitter says, 'That's it, it will never come, I can't finish this, I'm not good enough.', but the persistent (stubborn+optimistic) person says in that moment, 'Not yet, I'm going to try just a little bit longer, I think I might be able to figure this out.'

It may take thousands of those tiny moments for the persistent person to finish, but that is really the difference.

Sean David Jenkins

DAY 247 You can learn great things from your mistakes when you aren't busy denying them.

DAY 248 When you stop chasing the wrong things you give the right things a chance to catch you.

DAY 249 Every single thing that has ever happened in your life is preparing you for a moment that is yet to come.

TRASH DUTY

Offer to help an elderly or disabled neighbor put the trash cans out on trash pickup day. It may not seem like much to you, but it will mean the world to the person you are helping. Be sure to go back and put the emptied trash cans back.

FAMILY GRATITUDE BOOK

Thanksgiving is a great time to do this, but you can do it *anytime*. Have everyone in the family (extended family included) write down the things they are grateful for – each on a separate sheet of paper. They can be BIG things or little things.

Younger children can draw pictures, put together collages, or whatever works.

When everyone has done it, compile everything into one scrapbook and create an Annual Family Gratitude Book. It is sure to become a family treasure!

> *And now we're going to talk about making a **POWERFUL WOMAN** difference on a larger scale – involving your workplace, your place of worship, or your neighborhood. I know you'll come up with the way that works best for you!* ☺

CONNECT WITH YOUR COMMUNITY

Create a council to work with community leaders to explore issues and make recommendations for change. You might do this through work, through your house of worship, or through your neighborhood association. Your community needs the benefit of many different perspectives.

DAY 250 There isn't anything noble about being superior to another person. True nobility is in being superior to the person you once were.

DAY 251 You will never become who you want to be if you keep blaming everyone else for who you are now.

_____

_____

_____

_____

_____

_____

_____

_____

_____

_____

_____

_____

_____

_____

_____

_____

_____

_____

_____

_____

_____

_____

_____

_____

_____

DAY 252   Don't listen to what people *say* – watch what they *do*.

366

DAY 253 Being alone does not mean you are lonely, and being lonely does not mean you are alone.

_____

_____

_____

_____

_____

_____

_____

_____

_____

_____

_____

_____

_____

_____

_____

_____

_____

_____

_____

_____

_____

_____

_____

_____

_____

_____

_____

_____

_____

_____

"Katie? Can you hear me?"
No answer.
"Katie? Katie? How are you feeling?"
No answer.
"Katie? Squeeze my hand if you can hear me."
Nothing.
"Well, I guess she's still too sedated. Let's give her 5-10 minutes and try again."
The postoperative nurses finished writing in Katie's chart and let her rest. Soon however, she was slightly conscious and trying to smile.

"Katie! Glad to see you. Can you hear me now?"
"Yes..." Katie whispered. Her throat was dry from the anesthesia.
She was all too familiar with hospitals, surgeries and their routines.

You see, Katie Prevas was born with *"epiphyseal dysplasia, a disease that causes your joints to overgrow and your bones to become immobile."* Although it only effects her left side, she also had scoliosis (or curvature of the spine). A rod surgically placed in her spine corrected the curve. By the year 2002, Katie had endured 20 surgeries...and she was only 17 years old.

Having a medical condition that made it impossible to wear high heels, walk without limping, play contact sports, or even sit cross-legged during a school assembly, has not stopped Katie. She insists on doing things her way.

"Sometimes, I have to remind myself that there are things I can't do--but still plenty I can do. I've figured out what my limits are and learned not to care about what other people expect my limits to be. I surprise a lot of people, even myself sometimes. The expectations people put on you really shouldn't matter--you need to set your own goals."

Katie is happy with her body and herself. Sure, she'd like to be "normal" (whatever that is), but she is not wasting time sitting around watching the world go by without her. She is involved with life and is definitely living it on her terms.

"Katie...how you feeling?" The nurse looked into Katie's bright lively eyes, a smile playing across her lips.

"I'm fine...just fine," came Katie's reply. *"When do I get out of here? I'm ready to go home now."*

I'm not worried about Katie. I can't imagine how much energy and stamina the girl would have without her disease. She will be fine. I am so glad she knows it, too. She says this of herself:

"Anyone who knows me knows I'm unstoppable and definitely unbreakable. And once I put my mind to something, you'd better watch out!"

I hope you are like that. *"Unstoppable!"*

If not, I encourage you today to take some beginning steps to getting that way. Determine that you won't quit until you've chased down all your dreams and made them reality!

Choose to become a POWERFUL WOMAN!

Love is not about sex, going on fancy dates, or showing off. It's about being with a person who makes you happy in a way nobody else can.

DAY 255 *Anyone can come into your life and say how much they love you. It takes someone really special to say in your life and show how much they love you.*

_____

_____

_____

_____

_____

_____

_____

_____

_____

_____

_____

_____

_____

_____

_____

_____

_____

_____

_____

_____

_____

_____

_____

_____

_____

_____

_____

_____

DAY 255 *Anyone can come into your life and say how much they love you. It*

DAY 256 *Love and appreciate your parents. We are often so busy growing up, we forget they are also growing old.*

BIKE SAFETY RODEO

Conduct a bike safety rodeo. Contact your local
law enforcement agency to help organize a bike
safety rodeo. Plan jointly with law enforcement and
medical personnel. Create an obstacle course and
address safety issues including riding instructions
and safety helmets. Maybe give free safety helmets
to attendees, as well as exploring other freebies
that are available. Ask the law enforcement agencies what they can provide.

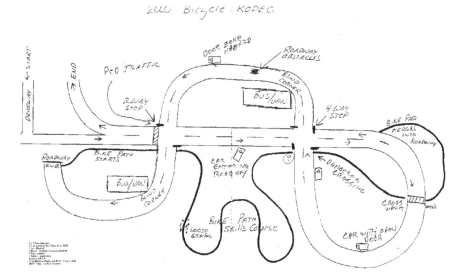

PARTY TIME!

Involve your neighborhood and community in block parties, section parties, or
park parties around themes. Some ideas: Earth Day;
connecting youth and elders; environmental issues, etc.
All of these can be collaborative projects to join neighbors
and community. Older teens can be given full
responsibility for the project – promoting leadership skills
at the same time they are creating change.

NATURE LABORATORY

Develop an outdoor nature laboratory working with the Nature Conservancy,
Department of Natural Resources and local officials for school and community
use. It is vital to life on Earth to increase awareness, understanding, and
appreciation of the world around us.

DAY 257 *When you have to start compromising yourself and your morals for the people around you, it's probably time to change the people around you.*

DAY 258 *Learn to love yourself first, instead of loving the idea of other people loving you.*

DAY 259 *When someone tells you, "You've changed," it might simply be because you've stopped living your life their way, and you're choosing to live it your way. Congratulations!*

_____
_____
_____
_____
_____
_____
_____
_____
_____
_____
_____
_____
_____
_____
_____
_____
_____
_____
_____
_____
_____
_____
_____
_____
_____
_____
_____
_____

"Hike! Hike"! called out the musher. *"Mush! Hike! All Right! Let's Go!"* The beautiful dog team responded to her commands and sprang into action . . . the team moving as one. The musher prepared herself for the racing speed of her team. The lead lines grew taut in her hands as her dogs set their pace.

The adrenaline coursed through her veins as the dogs began picking up speed.

It was her first time for the big race. Months of training, grueling exercises and many, many shorter races had her and her dogs in top physical and mental condition.

She knew she was ready. She knew her dogs were too.

Nothing remained between her and the finish line except... **over 1,150 miles of the roughest, most beautiful terrain on the planet**: jagged mountain ranges, frozen rivers, dense forests, desolate tundra and miles and miles of windswept coast. In addition, she knew temperatures would fall far below zero, winds could cause complete loss of visibility, there would be long hours of darkness and treacherous climbs.

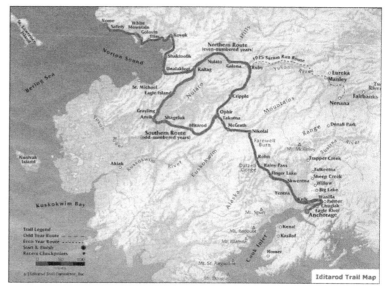

Iditarod Trail Map

It's known as the Last Great Race on Earth. It's a race run in Alaska by mushers and dogs. **It's the Iditarod.** Each team of 12 to 16 dogs, and their musher, will cover those 1150+ miles in 10 to 17 days.

The idea of the actual race was born in the mind of Dorothy G. Page, the "mother of the Iditarod."

The phone rang at Joe Redington's house one dark Alaskan evening. *"Hello."*

It was Dorothy. *"Joe, I have an idea. Why don't we start up the Iditarod trail again and make it a race? There's no excuse to let history die out. And don't you think mushers from around would come? I just can't sit back and watch that trail be lost anymore. We'll lose it forever if someone doesn't do something. Will you help me Joe? You're a musher, you know people. They'll listen to you. We can bring it back and keep it alive, don't you think?"*

Joe's answer, as history proves was a resounding YES! And he became known as the "Father of the Iditarod."

You see, Mrs. Page was an Alaskan historian who didn't want the Iditarod Trail, which had once been the major "thoroughfare" through Alaska, to be lost. By the mid 1960's most people in Alaska didn't even know there was an Iditarod Trail or that dog teams had played such an important part in Alaska's early settlement.

The Iditarod Trail has a rich history as a supply line from the coastal towns to the interior mining camps, and even beyond to the west coast communities of Alaska. Mail and supplies went in -- gold came out -- all by dog sled. Legends were born and heroes made. In 1925, part of that trail became a life-saving highway for Nome whose population was suffering from diphtheria. The serum was brought in by bravely determined mushers and their faithful life-saving, hard-driving dogs. Dorothy believed in the history of these people and their dogs, and desired to see their return.

Many believed it a crazy idea to send mushers into the vast uninhabited Alaskan wilderness. Many opposed this "race into death."

However, to date, over 400 finishers have come from Canada, Czechoslovakia, France, Great Britain, Germany, Norway, Switzerland, Italy, Japan, Austria, Australia, Sweden, the Soviet Union and from about 20 states in the U.S.

The list of participants, winning records and legends is pages long. Books have been written and movies made around the stories of trial and hardship, victory and success. Yet each person, and his or her dogs, have accomplished a feat few of us would even attempt. Each one of them has gone the distance and is part of the Iditarod legend. And these "legends" have Dorothy and Joe to thank – because they had a vision and put their passionate belief into action.

While most of us will never run such a grueling race, each of us faces challenges and difficulties. And each of us who attempts something new and different will be at the receiving end of comments like, "it'll never work," "you're crazy," and "give up before you make a fool of yourself."

But for those who decide to go the distance and never quit: pure satisfaction, boundless joy and a deep sense of fulfillment will be theirs.

You may have your own, personal Iditarod race to run. Don't give up! Give it your all and you, too can accomplish what you desire.

DAY 261 *No matter how good or bad you have it, wake up each day thankful for your life. Someone, somewhere else, is desperately fighting for theirs.*

Many people are truly poor because the only thing they have is money.

PENPAL OR EPAL CLUB

Create a PenPal or ePal club with community members and senior citizen centers. This is a great way to give the elderly members of your community a way to stay connected and not feel isolated and lonely. You'll be surprised how wonderful these relationships become to you.

Take it a step further... Gather a student group to develop PenPal or ePal relationships with other students all over the world. Set up an ePal relationship with a school in another country – getting a look into how other people live.

Besides being great fun, this is a way to develop relationships that will give you a place to visit when you're ready to travel – as well as you having the opportunity to host your PenPals that might come *your* direction!

COMMUNITY-WIDE CLEANUP

Offer to join with community officials and participate in fall and spring clean-up activities centering on safety, health and environmental issues. Develop brochures, leaflets, cards with safety tips to distribute throughout the community on cleanup day.

DAY 264   *When you choose to see the good in others, you end up finding the good in yourself.*

DAY 265 *It's better to know and be disappointed, than to never know and always wonder.*

DAY 266   *There are things we don't want to happen but have to accept, things we don't want to know but have to learn, and people we can't live without but have to let go.*

DAY 277 *If you tell the truth, it becomes a part of your past. If you lie, it becomes a part of your* future.

"You are good, Jennifer. I like your work. I think you'll go far in the cartoon world. I am putting your work out for display. Want to help?"

"Thanks, I would love to. But I have got to meet my mom. I have a doctor's appointment about my eyes. I'm nearly late now...can I do it tomorrow?"

The artist brushes and art paper jeered from the desk. Jennifer had just come from the doctor's office. She thought of all her dreams of being an artist, a cartoonist. She wondered if there were blind artists in the world.

She could not figure out what to do with herself. She was only 15 years old, yet she had dreamed many dreams. She was not quite blind yet. She had her whole life ahead. What would it be like to be blind? How would it feel? What would she do when her eyesight failed? How old would she be? How would her life turn out?

Several years later, and the scene is set like this. ...

Ladies and Gentleman, I would like to introduce you to award winning singer, best-selling Christian author, public speaker, motivator, and inspirational writer: Jennifer Rothschild.

As the applause grows, the curtain draws back revealing a woman dressed in white, smiling a beautiful smile. She sings words familiar to some in the crowd, "*It is well, with my soul.*"

Jennifer lives that truth...even as she struggled at first with her life; she has found peace within her soul with her blindness. She uses her unique position to offer hope to thousands at conferences and seminars across the USA.

"For me, blindness is a circumstance that opens the door to a host of other bewildering issues. One of the biggest daily realities I face is the stress of not being able to drive, read, or enjoy independence...Fear betrays; hope never does. Fear and despair make us quiver; hope makes us unshakable. Rather than giving into fear and despair, we tell our souls to hope. Hope will always be on your side, cheering you on and defending you."

Jennifer eventually set down her artist brushes, gave up the idea of becoming a commercial artist and picked up a microphone to speak and sing...inspiring the multitudes. She also picked up a pen to compose several best-selling books.

"Through her signature wit and poignant story-telling, audiences are prompted to look beyond their circumstances to find unique 'gifts,' in unusual packaging."

Jennifer didn't give up. Instead she refocused her life.

I want to do that too. Refocus whenever I need to.

You and I may not be battling a blinding illness but we battle many things that paralyze us from pursuing our dreams. Discouragement, depression, disillusionment...and even other people who try to stop us from dreaming...we face those every day.

Jennifer's advice?

"Steady, small actions will slowly reduce the big feeling that is paralyzing you. Just because you have failed at something does not mean you are a failure. If you quit, the world will be lacking what you alone bring to it."

This woman knows her stuff! She speaks wisdom when she says, *"If you quit, the world will be lacking what you alone bring to it."*

So don't quit. Stay at it for the long haul.

{ unknown }

Life is too short to wake up in the morning with regrets, so love the people who treat you right, forgive the ones who don't, and believe that everything happens for a reason.

DAY 278   *You can't start the next chapter of your life if you keep re-reading your last one.*

DAY 279 *Things turn out best for people who make the best out of the way things turn out.*

If you don't like something, change it. If you can't change it, change the way you think about it. You have total control of your choices...

PARTNER WITH BUSINESS AND INDUSTRY OFFICIALS

The time is coming when your kids will be deciding what they want to do with their life. Invite officials to the classroom, or to student organizations, or to the entire student body to share their business opportunity in the community; but more importantly what they as prospective employers expect from their employees and why.

Help them to make their presentation fun and exciting. Too many times these presentations are boring because many business leaders simply aren't speakers. *They certainly don't have to be.* Pull students into planning this. They know what will connect with their fellow students. The speakers will appreciate your help and input!

There is an amazing future waiting out there. Learn as much as you can about your options!

HOST A CRAFT MARKET/WORKSHOP

Invite the school community and residents to display their wares at a craft show. Ask participants to explain the why and the how they do what they do. At the end of the day, auction or sell products with proceeds going to a special cause.

Taking it further... Offer mini courses based on the interest in the different crafters. These courses will, of course, be offered to students but you can also offer them to adults – providing a course fee to compensate the artists for their time. If you do that they will probably be happy to do the courses for students at no charge.

Do good and feel good. Do bad and feel bad. It's that simple.

DAY 283 *Ultimately, it's not what you do every once in a while; it's what you dedicate yourself to on a regular basis that makes the difference.*

_____

_____

_____

_____

_____

_____

_____

_____

_____

_____

_____

_____

_____

_____

_____

_____

_____

_____

_____

_____

_____

_____

_____

_____

_____

_____

_____

_____

_____

_____

DAY 284 *Stay true to yourself. Never be ashamed of doing what feels right. Decide what you believe is right and stick to it.*

In 1931, Marguerite was only 3 when her daddy packed a suitcase and sent her and her 4 year old brother, Bailey, alone on the train to live with his mother.

"Daddy! I don't want to!"

"You have to. I can't take care of you right now! Granma Henderson will see after you. Now get on the train. Go with your brother!"

Four years later when Marguerite was 7, with no notice, he returned to usher the kids back to his estranged wife.

"Daddy! I don't want to leave!"

"You have to. Your mom will take care of you. Now let's go!"

One year later at age 8, Marguerite suffered sexual abuse at the hands of her mother's boyfriend. After confiding in Bailey what he had done to her, Bailey told the family how his sister had been violated. The boyfriend spent only one day in jail. However, he was found beaten to death just days after his release.

After that incident, when they were returned to Granma Henderson yet again, Marguerite didn't protest . . . she couldn't. Understandably traumatized, Marguerite internalized her pain and quit speaking. *"I thought if I spoke, my mouth would just issue out something that would kill people, randomly, so it was better not to talk."* Nearly five years would pass before she began speaking again.

A close friend and teacher, Bertha Flowers believed in Marguerite and simply loved her. Bertha introduced her to classic literature, and slowly coaxed her to speak again. The friendship stirred something within that young teenage girl. The literature would birth a passionate desire for all the arts within her, and Marguerite would spend decades experimenting with dance, speaking, drama, theater, and writing.

Her successes were slow and steady in coming; occurring between tragedy and heartache. You see, Marguerite also had a baby though she wasn't married; had a lover who forced her to work as a prostitute; married and divorced multiple times; and lost her son temporarily to a kidnapping. Many

things happened to her, and around her, that should have kept this woman from following her dreams. But she didn't let the obstacles stand in her way; she let them be stepping stones from which to learn.

You probably know her by her brother's nickname for Marguerite: Maya.

Maybe you've heard of her, Maya Angelou.

Her life story is not always easy to hear or as pretty as her acclaimed poetry. Tales of hardship, single motherhood, multiple marriages, and failed attempts at life interweave with tales of Broadway plays, foreign born husbands, exotic European and African homes, strong friendships with the likes of Martin Luther King, Malcolm X, James Baldwin and in later years, Roberta Flack, former U.S. President Bill Clinton, and Oprah Winfrey, among others.

Maya is a true Renaissance woman . . . billed as poet, dancer, producer, historian, playwright, director, best-selling author -- she still performs and speaks across the world. Now at age 80+, her public performances are billed at over $40,000 per engagement!!

Hard to believe that mute little girl has gone on to be the first African American woman to:

- operate a streetcar in San Francisco
- write an original script that was produced
- be featured in the *Poetry for Young People*
- write and recite her own work at a Presidential Inauguration

As an author and recording artist, she has over 40 books, plays, poetry compilations, and albums. Her television, radio, stage and theater credits, awards and national prizes are as numerous as her fifty honorary degrees from universities and colleges throughout the world.

I'd say she is a POWERFUL WOMAN! Wouldn't you?

Maya's life was far from easy – but it was out of the struggle and pain that she found her voice. It was slow in coming – but it came! There is no such thing as an "overnight success"!

Hold on! Believe that you will find your voice and you will!

Success is on the way if you will decide to never quit.

DAY 285 *No amount of money will make you happy if you're aren't happy with yourself.*

DAY 287 *You know you've made the right decision when there is peace in your heart.*

POWERFUL WOMAN ACTIONS

PUBLIC SPACES

Assist with developing a public space. Notice vacant lots, weedy parks, or ponds within the city limits. Work with officials and develop a plan of action to improve facilities.

GARDENING ANGELS

Invite students and personnel to volunteer to help community members develop and maintain small garden plots. This idea could be expanded to help provide fresh produce for Food Pantries in your town.

BE AN ENTREPRENEUR

Search for a business leader or industry leader that would mentor and work with your kid's school to establish a business within the school. Organize it in such a way that all students are involved - having responsibility to show ownership in the business. I.e.: popcorn business, candy business, flea market.

This is a powerful way to learn how to be an entrepreneur. You can set it up so that each student makes money AND puts money toward a special project you select as a group.

This is also a great way to learn about Internet Marketing. Find someone very successful and ask them to act as your mentor – for a whole group of students. Turn your computer into cash and learn valuable information. Search online to find the right person and then approach them via email or a phone call.

If you're thinking like everyone else, then you aren't thinking.

The unhappiest people in this world are the people who care most about what everyone else thinks.

_____

_____

_____

_____

_____

_____

_____

_____

_____

_____

_____

_____

_____

_____

_____

_____

_____

_____

_____

_____

_____

_____

_____

_____

_____

"But, Tetê, what will you do?"

"I'm not exactly sure, yet – that's why I'm going with you."

"Are you sure this is where you want to go – what you want to do?"

"Yes, I'm sure."

Maria Teresa Leal (better known as Tetê) was on her way to the home of her family's housekeeper. They were going to Rocinha, the largest *favela* (slum) in Rio de Janeiro. And she was on a mission.

Having been raised in a wealthy family in Rio de Janeiro, Brazil, Tetê was shown how to look beyond social and economic status and seek to serve others. She had been influenced by example. Her father, a leading physician, was one of the very first doctors to volunteer every Saturday in Rio's *favelas*. Her mother, a school teacher, encouraged her to expand her education to seek ways to give back to society. And her eldest sister started Rio's first Arts Education School to teach education and the arts to mixed classes of wealthy, middle-class **and** *favela* children.

Now it was Tetê's turn. Armed with a degree in Social Science and a license to teach elementary school, she was ready to make a difference.

Tetê knew that many women left their homes to do domestic work in the wealthy neighborhoods, or ended up in sweatshops, taking them away from

their children and their own homes. She also knew these women were famous for their sewing. So Tetê started a co-op for the women in Rocinha; now they could work at home and still bring in an income to help their families. They started by recycling fabric - creating quilts, pillows and rugs to sell at local fairs.

But Tetê wasn't satisfied. She knew these women were far more talented and skillful than what they were doing. When an international high-fashion show came to Rio de Janeiro, Tetê knew what she wanted to do. She wanted the women of Coopa-Roca (short for Women's Artisan and Seamstress Cooperative of Rocinha) to enter the world of high fashion. But there were a few hurdles to jump. First was the need for high quality fabric. So she secured donations of silk, linen and poplin – all fabrics unaffordable to her poor tailors.

Next she found fashion designers in Rio who donated their time and talent to teach the Coopa-Roca members the basics of clothing production. Reporters from *Elle* and *Vogue* magazines attended one of those training sessions. Tetê was encouraged.

Realizing they needed more exposure, she used fashion shows and national media to get the word out about Coopa-Roca's quality merchandise. They started participating in fashion shows and Tetê continued to get their products shown in the best fashion, lifestyle and home decorating magazines.

Knowing the skills (designing, cutting, sewing and finishing) is important, but Tetê has also made sure the women also learn about delivery, administration and publicity. Not only does the end result create a better paycheck, the women improve their math and language skills at the same time. Tetê has even created a program called, "The New Generation of Coopa-Roca" for young women aged 14-21 who receive special training in production techniques and management. New Generation is supported by UNESCO and the C&A Institute.

I'm so impressed with Tetê – aren't you? Just going into the largest slum of Rio de Janeiro and helping the women was a big thing. But to move them from quilts and pillows to international high-fashion is phenomenal. Can you imagine how wonderful it must be for these women to see their creations on super models and in international magazines?

Life is still difficult in the *favelas*. But the women are working for themselves, building up their self-esteem, and their sense of identity and pride.

You and I may never do what Tetê has done – but that's okay. Everyone's success looks different.

I know yours is going to look terrific! Here's to YOU!

DAY 292 *No one in the world was ever you before, with your particular gifts and abilities and possibilities.*

DAY 293 *A loving, happy person lives in a loving, happy world. A hateful, miserable person lives in a hateful, miserable world. The world around you reflects YOU.*

_____

_____

_____

_____

_____

_____

_____

_____

_____

_____

_____

_____

_____

_____

_____

_____

_____

_____

_____

_____

_____

_____

_____

_____

_____

_____

_____

_____

DAY 294 *Focus your conscious mind on things you desire, not things you fear.*
Doing so brings dreams to life.

VIDEO DOCUMENTARY

Create a video documentary with a group of young people. Determine subject, 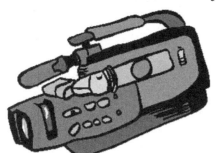 the timelines, age of participants, subject, and event(s). There is virtually no limit to what you and the kids can create a documentary on – your school, your community, environmental issues, animal issues – the list goes on and on... Choose a topic they are passionate about!

Distribute documentary to libraries, historical society, whomever. You may also want to have special viewings for students, families, etc. What about a documentary festival – with awards going to the top documentaries?

Taking the video documentary a little further... Have a "documentary contest" about needs in your community. The project will be about creating awareness of your community – inspiring students to want to help to make a difference. Invite the community to the awards ceremony – having booths available about how people can become involved to make a difference.

STUDENT STORE

Students can establish and run a store. Ask the school community to donate items to sell in the store. You'll be surprised how many will do this – especially when you put a sign on your store table saying who your donors are. It's great advertising for the business owners! It's also a great way for them to cull inventory and get a tax write-off on it.

There's no limit to what you can ask for... Determine the item's value, and  then market and sell it. Proceeds from the sale could be donated to a worthy cause.

This could be done in conjunction with carnivals, awareness days, etc. You'll be amazed how much you can make!

412

DAY 295 *To get something you've never had, you must do something you've never done.*

DAY 296   *The harder thing to do and the right thing to do are usually the same thing.*

DAY 298   *When you have two good options, always go with the one that scares you the most; because that is the one that's going to help you grow.*

"But it's just not right!"

"I agree, but the people don't know that."

"Someone needs to do something!"

"I believe I'm looking at that 'someone'!"

I imagine that conversation could have taken place between Nancy Kgengwenyane and her father.

Nancy was six months old when her parents divorced. She was raised by her father, a passionate man who loved Africa – all of Africa - not just their native Botswana. He taught Nancy she had a responsibility to Africa to develop her mind and use it on Africa's behalf. The school she attended nurtured this belief and the headmistress, who was a strong feminist, encouraged Nancy in all areas of her academic studies. Because she was fortunate enough to attend a school for white Zimbabwean children, her father underscored that enormous privilege also carried heavy responsibilities.

Upon completion of her studies, Nancy attended the University of Botswana to pursue the study of medicine, but the advanced math caused her to shift her attention from medicine to law. In her fourth year she was required to write a research paper which involved interviewing people in local villages. After visiting many villages and getting to know the people, Nancy became aware of the deep chasm between the law and the reality of people's lives.

Because of this first-hand knowledge, Nancy's focus shifted into a passionate desire to represent the needs of Botswana's people – especially women and children. Her work to raise the government's awareness caught the attention of the Attorney General who offered her a position in his office. Because of her quick intellect, her education among whites and her passion for Botswana and Africa as a whole, he transferred her to their New York City office.

While there she met environmental activists and became aware of the huge disparity between international and trade laws, and the realities of the people back home. Realizing how vital environmental issues are to Africa, she spent long hours volunteering after work. Her passion and commitment to this added dimension of her work became well known, and soon all pertinent environmental issues were referred to her.

Nancy resigned her post with the Attorney General's office and returned to Botswana. She started building grassroots support for legal reform and raising international awareness of the lopsided laws favoring multi-national corporations. She started a movement in Southern African that is the very first of its kind to challenge the industrialized world's definition of property and patent, and create an alternative that serves the developing world.

Dried Devil's Claw Root Herb

The issues are complex. For example -- there is

a root which is native to Botswana and Namibia called Devil's Claw. It provides relief for a variety of medical issues, including arthritis and gout. The root has been used for thousands of years by the indigenous people and is now being harvested by multi-national pharmaceutical companies. In some areas, the demand is so high that the root is over-harvested, and nothing is left for the traditional communities themselves.

These multi-national pharmaceutical companies have a huge profit margin, but return an extremely tiny percentage back to the native communities. Sometimes local villagers are paid a very meager amount to harvest the roots. These people do not know how to profit from their own resources and the multi-national companies use this to their advantage.

Nancy's goal is to establish within Botswana an organization that provides expertise and lobbying clout on legal and policy issues in the area of trade, biological diversity and intellectual property systems. Because of her work in the Attorney General's office, she has a wide network into which she is tapping. And that networking web continues to grow throughout Africa, Malaysia, Latin America, the U.S. and Europe.

Nancy has become a force to be reckoned with – and she is leading the way to save Africa from continued depletion of its natural resources.

Nancy was raised by a very wise father. He understood our intellect and abilities are not for our personal gain alone, but must always be used to help others along the way. His daughter is living proof that such a belief can make an enormous difference.

On your way to success, lift others and bring them along with you. The world will be a better place because you did – and so will you!

DAY 299 *Just because you don't understand something now doesn't mean the explanation doesn't exist.*

DAY 300 *Not knowing everything about your future is a good thing. It would probably scare you to death! But don't worry – you'll be ready for it when you get there.*

_____

_____

_____

_____

_____

_____

_____

_____

_____

_____

_____

_____

_____

_____

_____

_____

_____

_____

_____

_____

_____

_____

_____

_____

_____

_____

_____

DAY 300 *Not knowing everything about your future is a good thing. It would*

DAY 301 *The more you are in a state of gratitude, the more you will attract things to be grateful for.*

RECYCLING ANGEL

Develop a recycling plan for your work place and/or community. Ask the waste treatment officials to assist you in setting up a workable plan. You might decide to recycle paper. You will need to determine the kinds of bins necessary for different kinds of paper. Determine the value in recycling paper. You might want to collect plastic and or aluminum cans. This will demonstrate the value of recycling. It will also show cause and effect, savings and in some cases what to do with revenue generated from recycling.

BULLY PREVENTION

Take action to end bullying at your area schools. Besides standing up for anyone you know who is being bullied, you can work with your schools to bring Letters To Daddy – a fabulous musical about Bully-Prevention to your very own school – with your own drama club (or another drama club in the area) performing it.

Just go to www.LettersToDaddy.com to find out more and listen to some of the music. All the info is there about how your schools can get involved – with *you* leading the way!

GOLDEN AGE VOLUNTEERS

Encourage senior citizens to volunteer for projects and programs within the schools. Create a list of needs and conduct an Open House at a senior citizen center. Explain how they can help; storytelling, listen to groups read, read stories, tutor... The list goes on and on.

DAY 302 *It usually isn't what you have or where you are, or what you're doing that makes you happy. It's how you think about it all.*

DAY 303 *Do not dwell so much on creating your perfect life that you forget to live.*

DAY 304 *You are not in competition with anyone but yourself; plan to outdo your past, not other people.*

DAY 305 *To admit that you were wrong is to declare that you are wiser now than you were before.*

6-year-old Elvira looked up from her work in the fields. She was working beside her mother on her father's farm in Bolivia. *"Mama, why is Daddy so mean to those people?"*

"Don't look at them, Elvira, just do your work."

"Look Mama! Look!"

Elvira watched as one of the field hands escaped. She later learned her father had hunted him down, whipped him and hung him by chains in their basement.

Later that night, Elvira found her father's keys, slipped in quietly and invisibly into that dark, dank basement and freed the man. Young Elvira witnessed an atrocity that would never leave her. Those memories would carry her passion and zeal to right the wrongs of her society. Her courage came at a high price. Even though she was only a young girl, her father never spoke to her again – in fact, she was banished from her family and sent away.

Undaunted, Elvira Alvarez Ala grew up to carve a life as a staunch advocate for human rights and social justice.

Elvira didn't just see the injustices - she acted.

When her youngest child died because the local doctors refused to care for her family because they couldn't pay, she developed affordable public health care clinics so others wouldn't experience the same tragedy she had.

When she and her husband were working in an area where local miners sold their gold to an international mining company, she learned there was serious pollution of the drinking water because of the mining techniques. Elvira went to work publicizing what the mining company was doing. As you can imagine, this upset the mining company. It also made local doctors angry because their patients (who paid them in gold) were choosing to visit the new health care center Elvira's group was providing.

Elvira and her husband were accused of being subversive to the government and put into prison. Finally, after transferring to a woman's prison, a lawyer

and a Human Rights group quickly proved her innocence. During the seven months it took for her release, she organized the other women in the prison to demand visits to their spouses in the men's prison. Their demand was granted.

After her release, Elvira worked on getting her husband and newly-made friends out of prison. At that time, justice in Bolivia was delayed with serious violations of human rights.

In order to obtain bail, a prisoner had to put up a valuable piece of property such as a car or even their house. Most people simply did not have the resources to do that.

The law also required a rehabilitation program be in place *before* a prisoner would be released. Ironically, no such programs existed and people could spend months, even years in prison – waiting and forgotten.

Again, Elvira acted. She developed a process to help these abandoned prisoners. Her system included the prisoner, family members, friends and a sponsor pulling together to work through the necessary requirements so the prisoner could be released. She put together the steps a prisoner's advocate must take; how to create and propose a rehabilitation program and carry it out; how to develop a support system for the prisoner upon his or her release; and how the prisoner could get work once out of prison.

What an amazing life! From abandoned child, to health care activist, to prison reform advocate, Elvira Alvarez Ala has boldly stepped into the gap on the behalf of others. Her life has been all about helping those whose freedoms or rights have been taken.

Elvira chose to use what life handed her and successfully turn it around to make a difference in the lives of others. She is a prime example of one who found success because of determination and perseverance.

Like Elvira's, I hope your life will make a huge difference for others.

Elvira Alvarez in front of San Pedro Prison

If you wait to live your dreams, all that happens is you get older.

_____

_____

_____

_____

_____

_____

_____

_____

_____

_____

_____

_____

_____

_____

_____

_____

_____

_____

_____

_____

_____

_____

_____

_____

_____

_____

_____

_____

_____

DAY 308   *If you wait to live your dreams, all that happens is you get older.*

YOUTH KUDOS

Become a liaison between school and media. Make sure the media has all the "success stories" that happen daily in the schools. There is too much focus on the bad things youth do – let's put the focus on the great things they do!

WALL OF TRIBUTE

Create a "Wall of Tribute" for an area school. Work through the alumni association and community leaders to establish criteria for the wall. Recognize those in the school community who have gone beyond the norm in making a positive contribution to the community. This can be a tribute both to students, and the adults making a difference in the school.

Take this a step further and profile alumni who have done great things for the community and the world. Don't just put a picture – make sure you tell their story! Pride in your school will multiply when people see how many graduates have gone on to make a difference. It will also inspire others to make a difference so they will become part of the Wall of Tribute!

PARENT ENLIGHTENMENT

Parents really do care – they just need help in knowing how they can best help their kids – without embarrassing them or doing something stupid. ☺ Working closely with a group of students, develop a card or flyer with tips on how parents can foster their child's success in school and ask local employers about including the cards with employee paychecks. These could also be put in break rooms, etc.

Kids want their parents to understand them. Help be the Voice that tells them how to do it!

432

DAY 309 *I went for years without finishing anything. Because, of course, when you finish something you can be judged. What a waste... ~ Erica Jong*

DAY 310 *What is life? If is the flash of a firefly in the night. It is the breath of a buffalo in the wintertime. It is the little shadow which runs across the grass and loses itself in the sunset. ~ Crowfoot*

DAY 311 *I would rather be ashes than dust! I would rather that my spark burn out in a brilliant blaze than it be stifled by dry-rot. I would rather be a superb meteor, every atom of me in magnificent glow, than a sleepy and permanent planet. The function of a person is to LIVE, not to exist. I shall not waste my days trying to prolong them. I shall use my time. ~ Jack London*

DAY 312 *As you begin to live according to your own guidance and your own daring everything changes completely. ~ Leonard Willoughby*

"It's none of your business, Carolina!"

"But why not? If it affects my neighborhood, it affects me and it IS my business!"

"You don't understand, dear. It's just not how things are done – just don't get involved."

"That's not an option, Mother. I have to do something!"

Carolina Biquard's parents were raised in a country where the State took care of the community. She understood their hands-off mindset came from living under Argentinean dictators. But their passive mentality disturbed Carolina and fueled her desire to get involved and do something for her community.

After receiving her law degree, Carolina got involved with a project in Buenos Aires working with street children. The group's desire to build a better community, not just provide charity, impressed Carolina. She volunteered with the project for three years and then decided to abandon her career as a lawyer. Instead, she decided to *"become a human bridge between this project and the community."*

This head-strong, and compassionate woman became a pioneer in Argentina where non-profit organizations (NPOs) were basically ignored by the government and private sector. They were on their own. There was no organization, no networking, no collaboration between them, and no recognition or support. Carolina truly became a "human bridge," not only for the group she was helping – but for NPOs throughout Argentina.

Carolina's quest took her to the United States to learn more about non-profit organizations – how they work, how to raise funds, and how to raise community awareness about their services.

In 1992, Carolina was ready...

She began teaching courses in NPO management and fundraising at the local university. At the same time, she worked on her Master's Degree. Traveling to the U.S. several times during that period, Carolina attended seminars offered by the Drucker Foundation. She so impressed Peter Drucker (founder of the Foundation) that he became not only her mentor, but a dear friend until his death. (Much of their correspondence can be read online at the Claremont Graduate School's Graduate Center of Management archives.)

In 1994, Carolina created Fundación Compromiso ("Commitment Foundation") to help Argentinean NPOs organize, grow, and reach their potential as agents of social change. Her timing couldn't have been better. This was the missing key for the people of Argentina. The government had drastically cut back on services to the people. In response to the dire needs of the populace, a group of diverse NPOs stepped up to the plate to provide what the government had withdrawn. They were known as the "third sector."

But there was a problem – these NPOs were disorganized and struggling. Carolina's Fundación Compromiso filled the void by providing training for staff members and much-needed networking between the organizations. And the people of Argentina benefited because of her labor of love.

It's interesting, isn't it, that Carolina was raised in a family that taught her not to get involved in other people's lives? But her heart and head didn't accept what she was taught; deep inside she knew she had to do something. Carolina saw a huge void that needed filling. It took her several years before the idea of what she needed to do took shape. But when it did, she learned what she could, adapted it to her culture, and worked until her vision became reality.

What a great role model for you and me! I want to be like Carolina – don't you? When I see a hole in society that I know I can help fill, I want to have the same strength, courage, and conviction she had to do something about it, regardless of what people say. Carolina learned to be creative and "think outside the box," to adapt other people's ideas to her situation, and to come up with new and fresh methods to help people help others.

I hope you will think about Carolina today and decide to make a difference in your world. Don't be afraid to "think outside the box." Don't let others keep you from doing what you know in your heart-of-hearts you need to do.

Hold fast to your dreams and your determination and you will be a POWERFUL WOMAN!

DAY 313 *Don't walk behind me; I may not lead. Don't walk in front of me; I may not follow. Just walk beside me and be my friend.*

439

DAY 314   *To be yourself in a world that is constantly trying to make you something else is the greatest accomplishment. ~ Ralph Waldo Emerson*

COMMUNITY LIVING RESOURCES

Survey the community for living resources. Search for hidden talent from

Meeting Life's Challenges

members of the community that you can use in the classroom. Examples might be: something in the arts and crafts area; maybe in gourmet cooking; or something in the agriculture or science area. Develop a survey to find the talent that exists and then produce a booklet with contact information and areas of expertise. Make them available to schools and other organizations and agencies in the community to take advantage of the living resource. It will provide great benefits, as well as making people feel appreciated and needed.

COMMUNITY MURAL

Create and design a mural for your community. Explore the history of your

community and develop the mural accordingly. This is a great way to partner with local businesses whose walls will hold the mural. This could become an ongoing project with different classes creating different murals to highlight all parts of their community; showcase different time periods; etc.

Once a year hold a "Mural Walk" that will end with a celebration of your community at the school.

This is also a great way to enlist the help of local artists who can team up with the students to create them – providing a mentor relationship.

DAY 317 *Finish each day and be done with it. You have done what you could; some blunders and absurdities have crept in; forget them as soon as you can. Tomorrow is a new day; you shall begin it serenely and with too high a spirit to be encumbered with your old nonsense. ~ Emerson*

DAY 318 *Consult not your fears, but your hopes and dreams. Don't think about your frustrations, but about your unfilled potential. Don't be concerned with what you tried and failed, but with what it is still possible for you to do.*

Are you one of the nearly 22 million Americans who watch Dancing with the Stars? The year 2008 saw a special celebrity competing.

Want to guess how old she was? Try 82!

Dancing With The Stars is an American reality show. A celebrity teams up with a professional ballroom dancer and learns how to dance such dances as the foxtrot, cha-cha, waltz, samba and tango. They then perform live, and then three professional dance judges score their performance. Program viewers also vote electronically or over the phone. The lowest scoring team is asked to leave.

Hours and hours of work; learning, practicing, and performing are required. Muscle tone and fitness are required as well as agility and flexibility. Most contestants are young. They have to be.

Or do they?

Who was her competition on this dancing show? How about Olympic sports stars, professional football players, and actors *decades* younger. **Octogenarian** (someone in their 80s) Cloris Leachman dances her way across the stage with lights glaring and music swelling. Looking and acting decades younger, she recently completed work on three – yes – three films. In addition to the dance program, and those three films, she currently tours the U.S. with her one-woman show *CLORIS!* **and** is writing her memoirs.

Her schedule makes *me* tired!!

Cloris started out with a dream to be an actress. She began pursuing it in high school. She competed in the Miss America pageant (she was Miss Chicago) and won a scholarship she used to study acting in New York City. Her undergraduate college degree was in drama.

Cloris is one who knew what she wanted to do early. She simply put herself in the line of success by working her dreams. She's worked hard and often. She has taken the roles offered, and been available to try various genres and characters. She's been on Broadway, radio, TV programs, TV sitcoms, Hollywood movies, and has been a voice on animation films.

From the credits in her life; I counted over 60 films, 60 TV roles or appearances, and over 25 Emmys, Oscars, or Golden Globe awards. Actually, she's won over eight Emmys – more than any other female performer! That's a record! How awesome to be awarded for doing what you love.

Cloris created a niche for her talents and never swayed. Even at an age where many folks are fading, she is picking up speed!

Here's a key about dreaming – be consistent, stubborn and diligent.

Focus on the future and never let go of your dreams!

The future belongs to those who believe in the beauty of their dreams.
~ Eleanor Roosevelt

DAY 321 *Everything that is happening at this moment is a result of the choices you've made in the past.* ~Deepak Chopra

HELP A NON-PROFIT ORGANIZATION

NPO's always need to have more exposure, and many need help communicating their mission and their passion. YOU can help! Working with a marketing class (go to a local college or high school), artists create promotion promotional brochures, displays, videos, photo journal, etc, for a non-profit agency you're excited about. You, and everyone involved, will be able to see their efforts make a difference in their community.

LIVING HISTORY

Connect generations and experiences. Put together groups of friends and students to visit nursing homes, rehabs, veteran's hospitals, etc. to collect and document what life was like during major recent historical periods. Their reports can be written, photographed, and videoed.

They will become valued resources for families, friends, your school, your local library & your local historical society. Your paper may even publish some of your reports.

Along the way, you and your friends will learn that history is nothing more than stories of how people have lived their lives! It's not boring – it's alive and exciting!

NOT JUST HUNGRY ON THE HOLIDAYS

Use the holidays to help families, but "extend the giving". Keep food bins in

your office or place of worship to collect food for 2 families. Once every couple weeks take the food to the families. If families are hungry at the holidays, they are going to be hungry *year round*. Your leadership in creating ongoing giving can make a huge difference.

You will never possess what you are unwilling to pursue.

DAY 324   *Physical fitness is not only one of the most important keys to a healthy body; it is the basis of dynamic and creative intellectual activity.*

453

The infant's first cries were strangely out of place. Not in a hospital, not in her parent's home... little Gabrielle was born in the French poorhouse where her mother worked. She didn't remember that, of course, but six years later she did remember the fear and bewilderment when her father abandoned her and her four siblings when her mother died.

"Where did Daddy go? Where's Mama?"

"I don't want to go there – I want to go home!"

*"The orphanage **is** your new home, Gabrielle. I'm sorry, but you have no other place to go."*

At 6 years of age, Gabrielle's world tumbled down around her. With no family to take her in, she became a ward of the state and was placed in a Catholic orphanage. This would be home for the next 11 years.

When Gabrielle turned 17 she was moved to another convent school. The nuns there found work for her as a seamstress. But Gabrielle left that job for a brief career as a cabaret (café) and concert singer and adopted the name Coco.

The year was 1910, and it didn't take long for Coco to make the move to the big city of Paris and secure financing for her first business – making women's hats. She expanded from hats to clothing, and moved to the French sea coast resort towns. Her radical clothing designs were eagerly adopted.

Coco's free lifestyle was reflected in her rejection of the women's clothing of the time that included tight-fitting corsets, long dresses, and petticoats. She threw all that out and moved to a relaxed, comfortable, simple fashion, with short skirts and a casual look. She introduced a simple daytime suit for women, and pioneered "costume" jewelry by wearing multiple strands of pearls or gold chains. She also introduced heavily sequined evening attire.

Always seeking comfort in her styles, Coco took the soft Jersey fabric (then used for men's underwear), and created the first relaxed, sports clothing for women. She also used this fabric for her suits.

But it was her signature perfume that made her a millionaire – Chanel No. 5 was the first-ever scent that carried the name of its designer. Of her perfume, Chanel said, *"This perfume is not just beautiful and fragrant. It contains my blood and sweat and a million broken dreams."*

Out of a sad, tragic beginning, Gabrielle "Coco" Chanel carved out her unique one-of-a-kind genius and created a revolution in women's clothing. Her simple, elegant designs transcend the decades and remain the basics of good taste, fashion and design.

Like Coco, you are unique and have your own special genius – you just need to discover and embrace it! Don't be afraid to look at things differently. Think outside the box.

Encourage "the child" within you, and embrace the spontaneity and specialness that is exclusively YOU!

Let **your** special genius shrine through!

IN
ORDER
TO BE
IRREPLACEABLE,
ONE MUST
ALWAYS
BE DIFFERENT.

—COCO CHANEL

DAY 327   *Life expectancy would grow by leaps and bounds if green vegetables smelled as good as bacon. ~ Doug Larson*

DAY 328 *I'm sick of the food industry thinking they can pile garbage into my body just because they believe I'm a stupid teenager who doesn't care about my health. Nonsense! I will make good choices every day! ~ Mandy Wilkins*

_____
_____
_____
_____
_____
_____
_____
_____
_____
_____
_____
_____
_____
_____
_____
_____
_____
_____
_____
_____
_____
_____
_____
_____
_____

DAY 329   *Take care of your body. It's the only place you have to live.*
          ~ Jim Rohn

KID TO KID VIDEOS

This can be a really fun one to do because every single young person experiences this – and you can make it better for them! Make the transition from elementary to middle school to high school less scary. Dispel those ugly rumors by creating Kids to Kids videos that addresses the very special questions and fears that kids have about moving from school to school. These are a great way to reduce those fears and anxieties.

Just get together a group of upper-classmen (no matter what type of school) and ask them to share their experiences on video – giving advice to kids who are just starting out. This is POWERFUL!

NATIONAL YOUTH SERVICE DAY

Go online to www.ysa.org and learn about National Youth Service Day.

Complete the application and study the guidelines. Then connect area students with students across the county to serve their community by giving back. Have them enter the competition and become Nationally Recognized for their efforts.

Enter the competition school-wide with a group of your friends, and really make a splash!

DAY 332 *Don't eat anything your great-great grandmother wouldn't recognize as food. There are a great many food-like items in the supermarket your ancestors wouldn't recognize as food. Stay away from them!*

DAY 333 *Today, more than 95% of all chronic disease is caused by food choice, toxic food ingredients, nutritional deficiencies and lack of physical exercise. I'm proving to my friends I can make better choices than most teenagers do.*

_____

_____

_____

_____

_____

_____

_____

_____

_____

_____

_____

_____

_____

_____

_____

_____

_____

_____

_____

_____

_____

_____

_____

_____

_____

_____

_____

DAY 333

She took her place at the table. It was another Friday night concert somewhere in the middle of the United States. Thousands of people were streaming to their seats. Concert time was more than an hour away, but *crowded* was the only word to describe the walkway between the entrances.

"T-shirts! T-shirts! Garth Brooks T-shirts! Get 'em and wear 'em to the show!"

"Garth Brooks hats! Wear 'em like he does!"

At the end of the night, a weary Martina met up with her husband, John. She smiled as she watched him stride up the stairs. He had worked the concert too, 'mixing' sound. In fact, she had taken this job to be with John. She had grown so tired of staying home alone when he travelled. The one semester of college she had attended, staying behind at home, hadn't suited her at all.

Now she was hawking fan gear for a major country star.

Selling t-shirts had been the only job vacancy. She enjoyed the contact with his fans. Her own dreams, however, would take her to the stage as well. At least she hoped they would.

This show over, she exhaled. Sitting in the corner chair of their hotel room, she dialed her parents. Wanting to connect with her roots, she reminisced. Years of family bands, family concerts, and local dance stages drifted back to her. She came from a small town in the middle of nowhere Kansas. The "local" venues where she sang were a *very* far cry from the starlight of the capital of country music -- Nashville, Tennessee. Her small, but appreciative, audiences were usually made up of many family and friends.

Hanging up from chatting with her folks, she turned to John as he readied for bed.

"Hey, honey, I heard from a friend tonight that RCA is looking to add another female voice to its roster. Know anyone over there?"

"No, babe, I don't. They won't listen to unrequested material, either. That I do know. It's only a small obstacle. We'll figure out something. We gotta get your voice heard down there. You should be singing...."

"Well, what do you have in mind?"

John and Martina creatively placed her photos, biography, and 2 demo tapes in a large purple envelope addressed to RCA records with the **bogus** words "Requested Material." It worked!

Just a few short weeks later, she had both a record deal with RCA and a new job with country music super-star, Garth Brooks, as *his opening act!*

This, my friends, is Martina McBride. Her gorgeous voice went from nowhere, to being awarded *Top Female Vocalist, Favorite Female Country Artist, Female Video of the Year or Female Vocalist of the Year* ten different times between the years of 1999 and 2004!

Her creativity in drawing attention to her voice created the venue in which her dreams materialized. The stage became her home. Her husband, John, created and owns one of the top concert sound companies in the music industry.

Did she have a college degree in music? *Nope.*

Did she have the 'right' family? *Nope.*

She simply contented herself with selling shirts as she *waited* for her time to come. Never giving up. Never quitting. Always looking ahead to what could be.

Then Martina pushed just a bit with that purple envelope, edging out her competition. By believing in her dreams she knew she had nothing to lose and everything to gain by being different.

Today may you be encouraged by Martina's story, her life, and her belief in her dreams.

I encourage you to dream today, and every day. One day you may see those dreams come true! (The opposite is true as well. If you don't have dreams, they sure can't come true, now can they?)

So dream them and work them – anyway!

DAY 335 *I've come to believe that all my past failure and frustrations were actually laying the foundation for the understandings that have created the new level of living I now enjoy.* ~ Anthony Robbins

No matter how hard the past, you can always begin again. ~ Buddha

TOUCH AMERICA PROJECT

If you know kids who like being outdoors they will love the Touch America Project – and so will their friends! This program is designed for youth ages 14-17. They can volunteer and learn more about America's natural resources. "Touch America" refers to volunteer projects on public lands developed cooperatively with private organizations, groups or individuals. Encourage outdoor oriented students to learn more about wildlife and natural resources by checking out this and other programs offered through the National Forest Service.

Anyone who gets involved can bring back their newfound knowledge, and share their experiences with peers and organizations within your community. All of them gain recognition, but most importantly, they have the opportunity to get others involved.

THE YOUTH CONSERVATION CORPS

www.thesca.org/con_corps.cfm. This is a great program for youth ages 15-18 who work, learn and earn together on projects that further the development and conservation of the natural resources of the United States. This program is sponsored through the National Park Service. Conservation work may involve constructing trails, campground facilities and fences, planting trees, collecting litter, clearing streams, improving wildlife habitat, providing information to visitors and general maintenance activities. Students return with the knowledge of a job well done that makes a difference in our country, as well as knowledge of our environment and the management of our natural resources.

ARCHEOLOGY ANYONE??

If you or some of your friends are interested in archeology, contact the U.S. Forest service and find out the requirements to participate in this program with professional archaeologist and historians on historic preservation projects. www.fs.fed.us

DAY 337   *Nothing that has happened in your past can define who you choose to be TODAY.*   *~ Ginny Dye*

DAY 338 *There are only 2 ways to live your life. One is as though nothing is a miracle. The other is as if everything is. ~Albert Einstein*

All that we are is the result of what we have thought. ~ Buddha

"Lola, you've got to stop this insanity!"

"I'm sorry you feel that way."

"You're embarrassing your husband and family – you MUST stop!"

"I will never stop. Please give my love to Father."

I can only imagine that such a conversation took place between this courageous woman and a well-meaning friend or family member. Movies are made from stories like Lola's!

Born into a wealthy Ecuadorian family, Lola Samaniego Idrovo had every advantage. But desire for the finer things in life took a backseat for her because of the teachings of her doctor-grandfather who was deeply involved in issues of social justice and poverty. Her empathy for those who suffered resulted in her majoring in anthropology at the university. Intense pressure and criticism from family, her ex-husband, and wealthy peers, only fueled her passion to help the poorest of the poor.

After graduating, Lola worked in Chile, Brazil, and Ecuador, promoting human rights. She observed first-hand the dire situation of women who had been deserted by their husbands. Men were leaving their families in growing numbers every year. They were seeking employment in different regions of the country, or leaving Ecuador altogether, and never coming back. Women were left with little or no income or resources to help put their lives back together.

In rural areas, women were often forced to leave their land and move to cities in search of work so they could provide for their families. They usually ended up living in slums and finding themselves in even worse predicaments. Families lived in dark, one-room cement block homes (about 90 square feet) with no access to basic services or a yard. The block houses created a cold cement world which forced them into a vicious cycle of bitterness, shame, inability to provide for their families, and further desperation.

When eight women with whom Lola was working approached her about their particular situations, her work experience and creativity kicked in. What if they could band together and create their own village? Lola contacted 178 of the poorest families in the

476

area with her idea – she called it an urban village.

The families formed an association and under Lola's guidance started planning. Their village would be near a large city for access to services, markets, and schools. They would pool their incomes to purchase land so they would be true land owners and not just another group receiving government handouts.

Unlike the typical concrete block structures, houses would be attractive, comfortable, and sit on a small plot of land for private gardens. There would also be a community orchard. Members would help each other build their homes, and they would construct a public center for education, community meetings, and recreation. Care would be taken to maintain the ecology of the land.

Within five months of the association's establishment, the members purchased five acres.

Lola has also developed a leadership team of 25 women whom she trains and works alongside. Not only is the urban village changing the quality of people's lives, the process is changing individual lives as well.

Lola is determined to extend this urban village model throughout Ecuador, as well as other countries around the world. She envisions an entire global network of urban villages working together to share best practices and lessons learned.

You know what's really amazing about Lola? She believes in her model so much that she has actually left her family and moved into the urban village. Her wealthy family and friends can't understand her.

It's important to surround yourself with people who are positive and supportive – people who will encourage you to reach your full potential. These will be people who sometimes challenge you and make you evaluate where you are, with where you *want* to be. They will hold you accountable for your actions. They will help you move forward and not allow you to stand still and get stagnant, complacent, or apathetic.

Be like Lola, and go after your dreams, regardless of what others think or say. Be true to your heart. Embrace your passion. Live without regret or compromise.

DAY 342 *You gain strength, courage and confidence by every experience in which you really stop to look fear in the face. You must do the thing you think you cannot do. ~ Eleanor Roosevelt*

DAY 343 *Learn from yesterday, live for today, hope for tomorrow. The important thing is to not stop questioning. ~ Albert Einstein*

POWERFUL WOMAN ACTIONS

SCAVENGER HUNT!

Plan this for your work place, neighborhood, or place of worship. Have a Special Scavenger Hunt. Organize a scavenger hunt for specific items for different organizations. The Crisis Center for women and children could use toys, old cell phones, paper goods, clothes. Collect eyeglasses for the Lions Club. Pet food for the Humane Society. And the list goes on and on. Have prizes for the winning team and you'll have great involvement!

RECYCLE TOYS

First you collect old toys from all your friends. Ask the community to donate toys for the needy, or for various shelters. You could even make this the focus of one of the Scavenger Hunt groups from above...

It will be easy to gather SO many toys! Then you need to find interested students and patrons who will assist in repairing and refurbishing them.

Pass them out to the local shelters and anywhere else that provides support for families with children. These are common at Christmas time, but don't kids want and need toys year round??

QUILTING

Do you have friends interested in Quilting? Team up with the local quilting group. Design, cut and sew pieces for the quilt. Sell the finished product for a particular cause at a community auction.

This is a great way to join generations. You can also have adults work with students to create a special "Student Quilt" that can be raffled for a worthy cause.

If you've lost an area student you can make a memory quilt. Or start a tradition at your area school of making a quilt that highlights the events of your senior year – and then display them on a large wall.

DAY 344 *The whole secret of a successful life is to find out what is one's destiny to do, and then do it. ~ Henry Ford*

DAY 346 *Seize the moment of excited curiosity on any subject to solve your doubts; for if you let it pass, the desire may never return, and you may remain in ignorance. ~ William Wirt*

What you are is what you have been, and what you will be is what you do now. ~ Buddha

POWERFUL WOMAN STORY
Tenacious Dreamer

This woman's life reads like one of her novels. These fact-based excerpts represent her real life; after you've read them, you'll discover who she is and why you probably have read her works.

Ready?

Let's read on!

"Come to dinner, honey!"

"Be right there...in a minute," the 7 year old called to her mom. *"Just gotta finish writing in my journal."* She said it more to herself as she turned back to her writing. She wrote, *"Nothing much happened today."* Satisfied, she flung her notebook under her bed, hidden from her siblings, and scurried to dinner.

"Mama, what is a 'depression'? Why are those people standing in line for food?"

"Mama, why did Daddy die? He was just sleeping. I don't understand."

"Mama, I don't care if they pay us. I don't like them. I don't like the boarders that live with us. I want my room back!"

"Mama, my brother is not dead! Joseph will get better. You'll see, he is not dead. Quit saying that, he is not dead!"

"It's another rejection notice. They don't want my writing."

"It's another rejection notice...they don't want my writing."

"It's another rejection notice...they still don't want my writing."

"It's been 6 years and 40 rejection slips! But I am not quitting. One day, they will publish my works."

A grown woman now, with five children of her own, the aspiring author had worked as a secretary, a switchboard operator, a catalogue model, and airline flight attendant. She continued her education and her writing through all the tough events of her life. Yet, the hardest times were still ahead. She lost both her husband and his mother on the same night. Suddenly she was widowed, and her children were fatherless.

With those deaths, there was much to overcome.

Still she wrote. She never quit.

She wrote short stories, radio programs, and catalogue copy. She worked

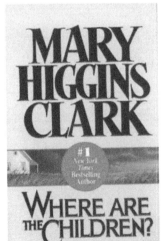

hard to see her dreams come true. Finally, after many attempts to publish, she received word in April 1974 that her novel, *Where Are The Children* had been accepted for publication! Success! Her payment of $3000 was quite a meager sum for a novel.

Nevertheless, it was a start.

Best of all -- no rejection notice!

Then 3 months later, the paperback rights to that book sold and her payment soared to $100,000!!!

WOW! What an increase, huh?

It gets better. In 1976, just two short years later, her second novel sold for $1.5 million!

The rest as they say *"is history."*

The woman I am talking about is Mary Higgins Clark.

She has published 24 suspense novels. EACH book is a bestseller in the U.S. and in Europe.

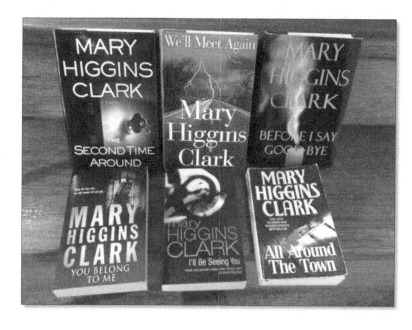

Did you catch that? After 6 years and 40 rejections, every suspense novel she has written became a best seller!

Phenomenal!

Moreover, even today, *all of her novels remain in print*. Her debut suspense novel, *Where Are The Children*, is in its seventy-fifth printing! That is an amazing feat!

She has written children's books, co-authored books with her daughter, and done non-fiction works. Numerous books became television films, and four were made into full screen movies. She is, at 80 years of age, the Number One best-selling fiction author in France, and recently began working on yet another book.

I hope I am that stubborn and tenacious with my own dreams. I hope you are, too. Keep trying. Keep at it!!

I encourage you to do the same. Keep on. You can live your dreams too, if you don't quit!

DAY 348 When you want to succeed as bad as you want to breathe, then you'll be successful ~ Eric Thomas

DAY 349   As long as you're going to be thinking anyway, think BIG.
~ Donald Trump

DAY 350 If your ship doesn't come in; swim out to meet it.
~ Jonathan Winters

The rest of the Powerful Woman Actions are going to be about taking care of your home – the Earth! Generations before you have left you quite a challenge, but with the right actions, I believe it's possible to save this amazing planet we all call home. Thank you!

STOP JUNK MAIL

Have you ever considered how much energy is used in creating all that
unsolicited junk your family gets in your mailbox? It's been suggested that the junk mail we Americans receive in just one day is not only a nuisance; it could produce enough energy to heat a quarter of a million homes! The junk mail delivered to *your* address alone would be the equivalent of 1½ trees – which adds up to 100 million trees every year. And that's just  in the United States. To help stop junk mail and help your letter carrier's aching back, write to: Mail Preference Service, Direct Marketing Association, P.O. Box 3861, New York, NY 10163-3861. By writing them you can reduce your junk mail by up to 75%. Be sure to recycle the rest!

RECYCLE!

Lead the way in making sure your household recycles. Participate in your community's curbside recycling. Make the effort to use those recycle bins!

Some communities are starting to charge fines to people who are throwing away items that should be recycled. And if your community doesn't pick up recyclables (or only certain ones) you can usually find someone who accepts them. Check with dry cleaners, supermarkets, manufacturers, your local public works department and civic organizations to find where recycled goods can be dropped off.

The only place where success comes before work is in the dictionary.
~ Vidal Sassoon

DAY 352 I've missed more than 9000 shots in my career. I've lost almost 300 games. 26 times, I've been trusted to take the game winning shot and missed. I've failed over and over again in my life. And that is why I succeed.
~ Michael Jordan

DAY 353 Get going. Move forward. Aim High. Plan a take-off. Don't just sit on the runway and hope someone will come along and push the airplane. It simply won't happen. Change your attitude and gain some altitude. Believe me, you'll love it up here. ~ Donald Trump

The nine brothers and sisters huddled together.

"Ok, it's decided then, right?"

"Right!"

"When one of us gets to the university, he or she will help the next one get there. Right?"

"Right!"

In many countries this idea wouldn't have been as big a deal as it was for Antonieta and her eight sisters and brothers. Born into a rural Mayan-Kaqchiukel family in Guatemala, it was rare enough for males to get an education – unheard of for females!

Life is anything but easy for the indigenous people of Central America. In Guatemala more than 50% of the poor, rural, primarily indigenous population lacks even the most basic of services (including schools) and only 7% of their homes have access to telephones, radios, or other communication.

Indigenous women in particular live on the outside edge of society. They do not have the same opportunities as men to study, learn Spanish, leave their communities, and improve themselves; much less serve in public office. They are mistreated within their own communities by being forced into servitude to their husbands. In addition, because they often live in extreme poverty, women must concentrate on feeding their families with little or no thought to their own needs or rights.

But with the help and support of her family, Antonieta Castro Abaj pushed her way out of this marginalized existence. Her parents encouraged all their children to study. And because of the pact the siblings made of helping each other get a college education, each one did attend university, and not one of them married before the age of 30. From extreme poverty to economic success, the Abaj family now has a veterinarian, doctor, teacher, pilot, and Antonieta - who is championing the cause of indigenous women in Guatemala and throughout Central America!

Antonieta knew all too well that the poorest of the poor didn't have time to think about human rights – they were too busy just trying to stay alive. So how could she help these people, especially the women who were at the very bottom rung of society? She knew she couldn't get them excited about their rights and possible escape from their dire situations with promises of freedom. It had to be something tangible, and it had to positively affect their husbands as well. What did they need the most? They needed money.

So Antonieta came up with a plan. She would offer women small, no-interest loans, and help them advance financially, **IF** they would attend one of her study groups. Antonieta went door-to-door recruiting women with the promise of financial help, if they would attend a special group she was offering just for them. It worked!

The study groups discuss pertinent issues ranging from local community issues, to national and even international politics. Through their discussions the women not only learn about their rights, but also develop interest in the politics of their local community and region.

And, as the women begin to bring in an additional income, their husbands and families encourage them to continue attending the study group.

Equipped with new knowledge and a new confidence, they are ready to get involved at the community level. Antonieta teaches them about the importance of having personal identification cards, and then helps them obtain them. With these cards, the women are then able to register to vote. She also encourages them to attend community meetings, and helps them contact the correct officials about their particular concerns. Finally, she encourages them to run for elected office.

While none of the first women who courageously sought political office were elected, they fostered hope, and set the precedence for others to follow.

Knowing she is only one woman who can do just so much, Antonieta trains the women who are members of the study groups how to recruit, start new groups, educate, and train even more women. Her simple approach is spreading throughout Guatemala and Central America.

Talk about a success story! Not only is Antonieta a public woman to be reckoned with; she is making a huge difference for marginalized people in her country, as well as throughout Central America. She is one who speaks with knowledge and authority, because she has already accomplished what she teaches others to do.

Wisdom comes from experience and is an integral part of success.

Remember Antonieta as you pursue your dreams!

497

DAY 355 *Life is short, fragile and does not wait for anyone. There will NEVER be a perfect time to pursue your dreams and goals.*

DAY 356 *Anything is possible. You can be told that you have a 90% chance, or a 50% chance, or a 1% chance, but you have to believe – and you have to fight.*

DAY 357 *Keep on going, and the chances are that you will stumble on something, perhaps when you are least expecting it. I never heard of anyone stumbling on something sitting down. ~ Charles F. Kettering*

PURCHASE CFC FREE PRODUCTS

CFC (chlorofluorocarbon) destroys the ozone layer which protects us from harmful UV rays. CFC's are used in air conditioners (as refrigerants/Freon), some scented candles, plug in air fresheners, insect repellents, hairspray, and even some cooking products. Most often they are in aerosol spray products. UV (harmful ultraviolet radiation) rays increase the risk of skin cancer, increases cataract cases, suppresses the human immune system, and cause environmental damage.

STOP PLASTIC BAGS!

Plastic bags are not biodegradable – they do not decompose fully. In addition, the ink is made up of cadmium and is highly toxic when released. Paper bags are reusable and biodegradable. Choose paper instead of plastic. Also – if your purchase is small enough, don't take a bag at all – this alone could save hundreds of millions of bags. Bring a cloth or string bag for smaller shopping

trips. You can also join other use who have helped to outlaw plastic bags in their area. That's the BEST way to eliminate their negative impact on our world.

USE RECHARGEABLE BATTERIES

Batteries contain heavy metals such as mercury and cadmium, which have become a major source of contamination in dumpsites. They break apart and are released into the soil or are incinerated and the deadly heavy metals are released into the air. Use batteries that are rechargeable. They will save you 10

or 20 times the original cost (by not buying batteries over and over again). You can also prolong the life of any battery by using the AC adapter for radios and other appliances. And recycle alkaline batteries if you can. The mercury and cadmium can be extracted for reuse.

DAY 360 *Life is not measured by the number of breaths we take, but by the moments that take our breath away.* ~ Maya Angelou

_____

_____

_____

_____

_____

_____

_____

_____

_____

_____

_____

_____

_____

_____

_____

_____

_____

_____

_____

_____

_____

_____

_____

_____

_____

_____

DAY 361 *Whatever you do, be different – that was the advice my mother gave me, and I can't think of better advice for a girl who wants to be powerful. If you're different, you will stand out.*

What did she feel? What did she want to do? She wanted to exclaim to the universe, to shout from the highest mountain, to proclaim to the ebbing ocean: *"The doctors were wrong! The doctors were wrong! Look at her now! There is no stopping her!"*

How fantastically good to know that being wrong sometimes feels so right!

Tracy Turner watched as her baby girl packed her belongings for college.

"College!" she thought to herself. *"Simply amazing, my baby is old enough to go to college!"*

Tracy knew Katelyn's dreams were becoming reality. It was incredible that Katelyn had even survived infancy. Tracy let her memory float back to Katelyn's birth and early childhood, and temporarily forgot the packing task in front of her.

As clothes flew out of the closet, Katelyn's excited chatter misted inside Tracy's mind as the memories of the horrifying diagnosis rose up.

Tracy remembered and silently rehearsed the telling of Katelyn's story....

"The doctors said she would die. Her spine didn't close during my pregnancy. It is called 'spina bifida.' Spina bifida means split spine. 'Bring her home and prepare for her death,' was the doctor's advice. Twice, they told her Katelyn would die. However, she didn't die...she thrived.

She learned to walk...then she hurt her toe. That infection first caused them to amputate five of her toes, then her foot and finally her leg. But Katelyn lived. She lived....Her dad, though couldn't handle the thought of a 'less than perfect' baby...he took one look at her and left all 4 of us ....just 3 months after her birth.

He only looked at her beautiful face one time. All the surgeries that she endured...If I count them...it is 56! 56 surgeries! How can one girl go through so much and still laugh and smile and care and dream? But look at her now!! How glorious that the doctors were so wrong!"

"MOM!" Katelyn raised her voice to seize her mother's attention. *"MOM! You are sitting on my new jeans...can you hand them to me please?"* Katelyn smiled and placed her hand on her mom's shoulder.

Katelyn Wilbanks is a dreamer and doesn't know the word "quit." When an infection forced the amputation of her leg, she learned to do more than just walk with her prosthetic leg. She learned to do back flips! She has such a contagious smile, and an overwhelmingly positive attitude, people are drawn to her as if she were magnetized.

A chance meeting with Mary Ann Zoellner, a producer of the TODAY show (an American TV show), led to a deep friendship between the two women. That friendship altered Katelyn's life.

When Mary Ann realized that due to medical bills Katelyn's family could not afford her "dream school" (the University of Oklahoma), Mary Ann stepped in to help find a way.

She believed in Katelyn's future.

Meetings and phone calls ensued between Mary Ann and the University of Oklahoma. As details finalized, the TODAY show flew Katelyn to a filming of the program under the pretext of "telling the world about spinal bifida." Much to her shocked surprise, the president of the university presented her with a full scholarship -- tuition, books, room, and board.

The grateful young woman inspired so much attention, the OU alumni association raised over $130 MILLION so others like her could attend the school!

As of 2008, Katelyn Wilbanks continues to attend the University of Oklahoma. Living in the athlete's dorm and working as a manager for the football team, she majors in journalism with a musical production minor. What started out as a common friendship has created tremendous success for one young woman and one large university.

"I chose Katelyn because there are certain people you meet in life that are angelic and take your breath away. Katelyn was one of those people for me," says Mary Ann.

OU President, David Boren says, the univeristy *"is going to be changed forever because she's here."*

Katelyn influences people everywhere with her gentle, positive spirit and her trademark smile. Never having had an easy time, she is passionate about life, and believes in her future against all odds.

"My mom said that after I was born I never had a will to die or give up. My mom didn't let the doctors' words give her a negative attitude. She never gave up, and neither did the rest of my family. I believe you should keep your head up whatever happens and everything will go your way. I've never let spina bifida get me down, I just use it as a stepping stone."

A stepping stone....minus one leg and a split spine...and she sees it is a stepping stone! WOW! I like this girl's attitude!

I want to be like Katelyn, ready to face whatever comes my way with a smile, my head held high, and a deep-seated resolve to succeed! AND I want to be a friend like Mary Ann and see the bright future of those around me.

What about you??

DAY 362 *A lot of people are afraid to say what they want. That's why they don't get what they want. ~ Madonna*

DAY 363 *I've come to believe that each of us has a personal calling that's as unique as a fingerprint – and that the best way to succeed is to discover what you love and then find a way to offer it to others in the form of service, working hard, and also allowing the energy of the universe to lead you. ~ Oprah Winfrey*

DAY 364 *A Powerful Woman understands that the gifts such as logic, decisiveness, and strength are just as feminine as intuition and emotional connection. She values and uses all her gifts. ~ Nancy Rathburn*

POWERFUL WOMAN STORY
She Was a Mahout

"Mom, Dad, I've decided to become a mahout."

*"Well dear, we have no doubt you'll become anything you want. You're going to be a **what**?"*

"A mahout – an elephant driver."

Caroline Casey is an achiever; actually most people would call her an over-achiever, because whatever she puts her Irish mind to, she accomplishes. Caroline was always a top student and excelled in college. She traveled extensively, founded a horticulture and landscape architecture business at the age of 22, and eventually became a successful business consultant to an international company.

But at the age of 28 she hit a corporate wall, and was unable to achieve at the high levels she was accustomed to. She quit work and decided to live out a life-long dream – riding an elephant across India. In fact, Caroline became the first western woman to achieve the status of elephant mahout. In 2000, she made the physically and mentally demanding 1000 kilometer trek (about 622 miles) across India.

But Caroline's story is not about being a celebrated elephant mahout. Her story is about the prejudice and difficulties she suffered (and overcame) as a result of being legally blind.

Growing up in Dublin, Caroline's friends laughed and joked about the clumsy kids who wore glasses. She didn't realize she had a vision problem until her parents bought her driving lessons. She couldn't pass the eye exam, and at the age of 17 was labeled visually impaired and legally blind. But Caroline and her parents hid her disability until she was 28 when she hit the corporate-world wall that changed her life.

Deciding to use her trip across India as a fundraiser and awareness raising venture, Caroline established The Aisling Foundation. She set the goal of raising EUR$250,000 (about $352,000 US) to support her trip **and** raise funding for various disability groups. A few weeks before the trip she had raised only had EUR$67,000. She managed to get a prime-time appearance on a national television talk show which enabled her to nearly double her goal -- EUR$480,000 (about $676,000 US)!

Caroline returned from her trip as an inspirational figure with a high media profile, and she took full advantage of it. She knew that almost 10 percent of Ireland's population lived with disabilities. 90 percent were unemployed and 38 percent lived in poverty. (By the way, these statistics hold true worldwide.)

While disability and rights groups had campaigned successfully for progressive legislation throughout Europe, businesses still resisted hiring employees with disabilities. Caroline knew first hand that like society in general, businesses see these people for what they cannot do instead of what they can. They also don't realize the spending power these individuals have.

Caroline decided to change how businesses look at, and deal with, people with disabilities.

She organized her first "ability conference" in 2001. Since then she has created The Ability Awards to recognize and reward businesses and public-sector organizations that strive to meet the needs of people with disabilities. These awards endeavor to make businesses and organizations "ability confident" as they meet the needs of employees ***and*** consumers.

The Ability Awards also target the government, people with disabilities and their families, educators, the media, and the general public. The televised awards are receiving more and more attention throughout Europe. The judging panels are made up of Ireland's leading business and citizen figures. It's interesting to note, that winning companies can only receive their award if the CEO or managing director is present on award night. This ensures that the issue of "ability" is recognized at the highest level.

But Caroline's vision goes beyond the awards. Her Foundation has also  created The Ability Program which is designed to systematically get the word out about best practices and industry standards that will ultimately empower more businesses. This Program is similar to the Chambers of Commerce model and provides training products, publications, conferences, and workshops.

Caroline's approach is based on innovation. Her Foundation is evolving into a research and development hub for ability programs. She envisions spreading these programs around the world by funding "ability agents" who will create a network of communities supporting one another. The Aisling Foundation will also help by providing financial, network, and best practice support.

Now that's one enterprising, energetic, young woman! She's gone from a 17-year-old hiding a disability, to a highly successful business consultant and business owner, to an elephant mahout trekking across India, to a CEO changing the world of business for people with disabilities. Amazing!

Caroline is a wonderful example of someone who refuses to let what others perceive as her limitations define who she is and what she can do. How often have you let someone's negative comment stop you from pursuing a great idea? Have you ever shared a dream with someone who told you to stop dreaming and face reality?

I encourage you to stay true to your dreams and turn a deaf ear to those who would try to talk you out of pursuing them.

This world needs positive, hard-working, energetic dreamers like Caroline – like YOU!

YOU'RE DONE!!

Your first **POWERFUL WOMAN JOURNAL** is complete!

It has been such a joy to share this year with you! I encourage you to keep your Journal as a treasure – a road map of your life. It's valuable to you right now; it will be just as valuable (or perhaps more) when you're older and are looking back at your life!

Are you ready for **POWERFUL WOMAN JOURNAL** # 2? If you've taken # 1 a day at a time, then #2 is waiting for you at: www.PowerfulWomanJournals.com

Again, you have 20 cover designs to choose from – only this time they were created by Powerful Women around the world – and chosen in a contest!

You'll also have 52 new Powerful Woman Stories... 100+ more ideas for making a difference in the world... 365 new empowering quotes...

And, yes, if you want your daughter, or other youth, in your life to have a Journal, we have one just for them – **THE POWERFUL GIRL JOURNAL**! Just go to www.PowerfulGirlJournals.com and order one for the special girls in your life!

Thank you for letting me be a part of your life for the last 12 months. It has been both an honor and a privilege!

Ginny Dye

Other Books by Ginny Dye

<u>Powerful Girl Journals – For Tween & Teens</u>

<u>The Bregdan Chronicles – Best-Selling Historical Fiction</u>

Storm Clouds Rolling In

On To Richmond

Spring Will Come

Dark Chaos

The Last, Long Night

Carried Forward By Hope

<u>When I Dream Series – for young children</u>

When I Dream, I Dream of Horses

When I Dream, I Dream of Puppies

When I Dream, I Dream of Snow

When I Dream, I Dream of Kittens

When I Dream, I Dream of Rabbits

When I Dream, I Dream of Elephants

When I Dream, I Dream of the Jungle

When I Dream, I Dream of the Ocean

When I Dream, I Dream of the Farm

And many more probably already in print!

<u>The Pepper Crest High Series – For Tweens & Teens</u>

Time For A Second Chance

It's Really A Matter of Trust

A Lost & Found Friend

Time For a Change of Heart

A Touch of Spring Fever

<u>The Nitty-Gritty Club Series</u> – For Tweens & Teens

<u>Fly To Your Dreams Series</u> – For All Ages

Dream Dragon

Born To Fly

Little Heart

The Miracle of Chinese Bamboo

<u>101+ Ways to Promote Your Business Opportunity</u>

<u>If You Want To Be A Success, Learn From 100+ People Who Already Are!</u>

All titles by Ginny Dye

www.AVoiceInTheWorld.com